# Your Daughters Shall Prophesy

# Your *Daughters* Shall Prophesy

A Living
Testament
of Perserverance
and Resilience in
the Midst of Life's
Disappointment

## DR. CLAUDIA BRANTLEY

ACW Press
Phoenix, Arizona 85013

**Your Daughters Shall Prophesy**
Copyright ©2002 Dr. Claudia P. Brantley
All rights reserved

Cover Design by Alpha Advertising
Interior design by Pine Hill Graphics

Packaged by ACW Press
5501 N. 7th Ave., #502
Phoenix, Arizona 85013
www.acwpress.com
The views expressed or implied in this work do not necessarily reflect those of ACW Press. Ultimate design, content, and editorial accuracy of this work is the responsibility of the author(s).

Library of Congress Cataloging-in-Publication Data
(Provided by Quality Books, Inc.)

Brantley, Claudia P.
    Your daughters shall prophesy / by Claudia P.
Brantley. -- 1st ed.
    p. cm.
    Includes bibliographical references.
    ISBN: 1-892525-80-1

    1. Brantley, Claudia P.  2. Women clergy.  3. Women
in church work.  4. Women clergy--Biblical teaching.
5. Women in church work--Biblical teaching.  I. Title.

BV676.B73 2002              262'.14
                           QBI02-200222

**Printed in the United States of America.**

"And it shall come to pass in the last days, saith God, I will pour out of my Spirit upon all flesh: and your sons and your daughters shall prophesy, and your young men shall see visions, and your old men shall dream dreams: And on my servants and on my handmaidens I will pour out in those days of my Spirit; and they shall prophesy."

Acts 2:17-18 (KJV) - Joel 2:28-29

# Dedication

Jesus Christ, my Savior and Lord

Hugh Hathorn Brantley, Jr.
My husband and best friend,

Our wonderful children and grandchildren,
Blessings from the Lord

Paul and Hope Brantley Cheshier
Ashley, Hunter, Marshall, Alainnah Cheshier

Bob and Dana Gossett Brantley
Robert Brantley

Paul and April Brantley VonWedel
Emma Grace VonWedel

and

Future grandchildren

# Acknowledgments

Special thanks are due to the following persons for their friendship and support during my ministerial journey thus far. I could not have made it without you and each of you know your part in my life. I love and appreciate you.

Dr. Sue Arledge, Presbyterian Minister, Cheraw, S.C.

Dr. John Blumenstein, Presbyterian Minister, Greenwood, S.C. (Previously a professor at Erskine Seminary).

Dr. Robert Culpepper, missionary in Japan and Professor of Theology, retired, Southeastern Seminary, Wake Forest, N. C.

Dr. Robert Hall, Professor, retired, Erskine Theological Seminary, Due West, S.C.

Dr. Merwyn Johnson, Professor, Erskine Theological Seminary, Due West, S.C.

Dr. Todd Jones, Pastor, First Presbyterian Church, Nashville, TN

Dr. Loyd Melton, Professor of Biblical Studies, Erskine Theological Seminary, Due West, S.C.

Reverend Robert Morgan, Associate Pastor, retired, First Baptist Church, Spartanburg, S.C.

Dr. Kirk Neely, Pastor, Morningside Baptist Church, Spartanburg, S.C.

Reverend Steven Rhodes, Pastor, Second Presbyterian Church, Spartanburg, S.C.

Dr. Bob Taylor, Executive Presbyter, retired, Foothills Presbytery

Dr. Alastair C. Walker, retired Pastor, First Baptist Church, Spartanburg, S.C.

Dr. George Wilkes, Executive Presbyter, Foothills Presbytery

Friends, too numerous to mentioned but never forgotten.
My Second Presbyterian Church family.

*In Memory*

*of*

**The Reverend Ronald Kenneth Wells**

*Beloved*

*Minister of Music*

*First Baptist Church*
*Spartanburg, South Carolina*

*Servant of God*

*Inspiration to Others*

# Contents

*Introduction*

✧

My growing up years were spent in a denomination that stressed the importance of receiving a call to serve God. So when I felt the call on my life to serve God as a minister, I did not expect to run into roadblocks.

As a child, I heard a minister preach from Numbers 22 in the Bible about Balaam's donkey and how God used the donkey to speak to Balaam. It was not until I answered God's call to the ministry that I realized some people would rather hear God speak through a donkey than through a woman. They did not take into account the prophecy in Joel and Acts that "your sons and *your daughters* shall prophesy (preach)."

Women in our society, seeking to obey the call to serve God, run into barricades that try to hold them back from doing what they feel God has called them to do. Obstacles are part of the ingredients of life. Everyone has them in one form or another.

When these obstacles become our companions, robbing us of our idealism and changing our perspectives, what happens in a person's life? Obstacles can either become stepping stones to maturity and revelations of God, or weights drowning us in an ocean of disillusionment, discouragement and depression.

The purpose for writing this book is three fold. First, in sharing the obstacles I encountered in a portion of my journey through life, and my responses, both negative and positive, I pray you will be able to touch God in your struggles, enabling Him to become more real and personal in your life. Although our circumstances may be different, the feelings and struggles we have amidst them, whatever they are, will be similar. You will identify with the emotions of pain, anger, resentment, discouragement, disillusionment, bitterness, betrayal and lowered self-esteem I experienced in my journey. May our Heavenly Father touch you in the obstacles encountered on your own spiritual journey through life, bringing comfort, insight and healing where they are needed. Most of all, may you experience a closer walk with God as you journey through this book.

Secondly, in sharing my ministerial journey, I pray men and women will be aware of the gross injustice dealt to women *called by God*. The pain and heartache they experience when denied a place of serving God affects every area of their lives.

Thirdly, during my struggles as a *woman in ministry*, there were no women mentors who came forth to help me down this path. It would have been helpful to communicate with another woman on a personal level who had already experienced what I was experiencing. Perhaps this book will be helpful to those who are making this ministerial journey.

I was blessed to have a husband, professors and a few pastors who mentored me and were supportive. I am grateful for each of them.

Hopefully in sharing some insight in a scholarly interpretation of biblical passages, in chapter 3, pages 37-49, *Biblical-Historical Background*, disputed in the controversy of *women in ministry*, people will be enlightened regarding these controversial passages.

Since this controversy is not one of the *essential doctrines* of the Bible, and there is room for differing interpretation, perhaps we can move on and maintain harmony and fellowship with one another even in our differences. "How good and pleasant it is when brothers [*and sisters*] live together in unity" (Psalm 133:1).

This story needs to be told. As I endured these heartbreaking experiences, there was not a network of women mentors, or books available to help me through my struggles. God's faithfulness brought me through. After the fact I saw that God had supplied the strength and determination to persevere amidst the obstacles. It would have been helpful to have had a female mentor, who had gone before, to show me the markers of hope along the way. May this book do that for those women who are seeking to follow God's call in ministry and for those who are experiencing hindrances in other fields of endeavor. They need to hear the voice of the Heavenly Father saying, "Continue to persevere. I am with you always and I will direct your paths."

### Perseverance

*One cold February day a snail started climbing an apple tree.*
*As he inched slowly upward, a worm stuck its head from a crevice*
*in the bark to offer some advice.*
*"You're wasting your energy. There isn't a single apple up there."*
*The snail kept up his slow climb.*
*"There will be when I get there," he said.*

—Anonymous

# Chapter One

# The Journey Begins

*"The Spirit of the Sovereign Lord is on me, because the Lord has anointed me to preach good news to the poor. He has sent me to bind up the brokenhearted, to proclaim freedom for the captives and release from darkness for the prisoners, to proclaim the year of the Lord's favor and the day of vengeance of our God, to comfort all who mourn..."*

Isaiah 61:1-2

One of my earliest memories as an elementary school girl in a small Southern town was being teased about my name. Some of the children would say things like, "Where is your Bible?" "What are you going to preach about on Sunday?" or "Here comes the Reverend."

They weren't being cruel, at least I didn't take it that way; they were just having fun at my expense, as children will do. Since I was a very shy child, I didn't vocalize the smart retorts I might have come up with at that stage of life. I would blush totally red and ignore them. After all, what could I say—my last name *was* "Preacher." I didn't realize, during those days, that name perhaps would be a little prophetic later in my life.

Actually, it was very much later this incident was brought back to my memory. At my ordination into the Presbyterian Church, USA as a minister, this memory clicked back into my consciousness. Perhaps I am getting ahead in my story. A lot happened before I reached the point of becoming a Presbyterian minister.

## A Backward Glance

A long awaited goal was just around the corner that beautiful spring day in May, 1965. My husband, Hugh, was about to graduate from Furman University with a Bachelor of Arts degree and a major in accounting. He had been hired at a bank in a nearby city and we were moving before the end of the summer to a *real house*. We had been living in a small apartment on campus with two very young children. Our children, Hope and Bob, were in a nursery while I worked full time. The plan, when we moved, was for me to be a "stay at home Mom" since Hugh had a full-time job.

The move to Spartanburg, South Carolina motivated us to look for a church to attend. Hugh and I attended church as high school students, but during the college years, religion took a back seat in our lives. We did not attend church except when we returned to our hometown to visit our parents, and then it was just to see our friends.

We began attending various churches in the area after we moved, and since we had been raised in the Southern Baptist denomination all the churches we visited were Southern Baptist. Finally, after a good many months we decided on a large Baptist church. Our reasons for joining the church were certainly not spiritual. This church had a softball team and my husband liked to play softball. It had a great choir and I liked to sing. The children's program was wonderful and we had two young children. So, one Sunday in the tradition of the Baptists, we walked down the aisle and joined the church by transfer of our letter. Hugh and I had both been baptized, he as a child and I as a teenager, so baptism wasn't necessary to join the church.

Since we had joined the church, we began attending Sunday School for the first time since our teen years. The men and women were divided into separate classes, so we attended different classes. My Sunday School teacher was a real student of the Bible, which she expounded to her class every Sunday. I found I enjoyed the classes but was very puzzled when she talked about Jesus as if He were a real person, someone alive today and involved in her daily life. One Sunday as my husband, children and I drove away from the church, I said, "Either I've got a crazy woman for a Sunday School teacher or I'm missing something." Well, at that point I really thought she was more crazy than I was missing anything.

We had been members of the church for about a year when I found out I was pregnant with our third child. As I lay in my hospital bed after she was born, I began to contemplate the conception, growth and birth of a baby. It was as if a lightbulb turned on in my head and illuminated this thought; "The birth of a baby is a miracle. There really has to be a God and I am going to find Him!" I did not realize at the time He was already there just waiting for me to acknowledge Him.

When our baby, April, was a month old, I decided I had to do something to *find God*.

Since I had been in the Baptist church all my life and felt I had missed God, I decided to talk with the Catholic priest in our area. The reason for this decision was because my sister-in-law, who had been raised Baptist, had joined the Catholic church while she attended a Catholic nursing school. The priest I contacted was gracious in answering questions and gave me literature to read concerning the Catholic church.

One Sunday I walked up to my Sunday School teacher in the Baptist church we were still attending and asked her, "Would you please pray for me? I am thinking about joining the Catholic church."

She said, "Darling, I've been praying for you for months." Well, that was a real turnoff to me at the time, but I kept going to her class because I felt drawn to the people and the teaching. I also had begun attending a home Bible study group where the Bible was being taught once a week. I was learning a lot about God through the Bible study as well. The historical Jesus was becoming more real.

The Baptist church used to have a Sunday night class called Training Union. The pastor who had been there for over twenty-five years retired, and a new pastor had just arrived. He was to speak in the Training Union department one Sunday evening. My sister was visiting me and we decided to attend Training Union and hear him speak. He was originally from another country and we liked his accent. He gave a testimony that evening about how he had become a Christian as a teenager and how God led him to America to attend college and seminary. He had married an American lady while in college and he became an American citizen. All his pastorates had been in the United States.

That night he spoke, just as my Sunday School teacher had, as if Jesus were a person involved in the daily events of his personal life. I knew he was sincere. This was disturbing to me because I knew I did not have this type of relationship with God and had begun to realize this as I attended Bible study and Sunday School.

The following Tuesday, the Baptist pastor and the Catholic priest, as well as members of the Baptist church, met in a church member's home. The purpose was for each clergyman to share what his denomination believed. They had been asked to do this by one of the Baptist church members because people had questions about the differences.

After the meeting was over I walked up to my pastor and said, "I don't believe I know Jesus Christ personally. Can you help me?"

He smiled real big and got very excited and said, "Yes, I can, when can I come to your home to talk with you?" He wrote down my name and address and made an appointment to come out on Thursday evening to talk to Hugh and me. I had two days to wait.

Thursday evening arrived. I was nervous but excited. Seven-thirty came and went and no pastor. After about thirty minutes I sat on the front steps of my home and cried and told God, "I won't have anything else to do with church, religion, pastors or the Bible." I was not saying this calmly or quietly.

My husband said very calmly, "Claudia, something probably happened and he will call tomorrow." I would not be comforted because I was so upset about his not coming. I had high expectations I would find some answers if he had just come.

The next morning, I was in a very emotional state. I did not understand then the phrase of "someone being under conviction because the Holy Spirit was drawing them to the Father." I just knew I felt miserable. I picked up the phone and dialed the pastor's church office at 8:00 A.M. and he answered the phone. I said, "This is Claudia…."

The pastor interrupted before I could say anything else and said, "Claudia, I am so glad you called. I lost the paper with your name and address and all I could remember was your first name. When can I talk with you?"

We were leaving that day to go on vacation and I was so distraught, I knew I could not leave without settling whatever was going on within me. So I said, "I can come at 1:00 P.M. today." He said, "I will look forward to seeing you then."

Those five hours were so slow but the time finally arrived. The pastor talked with me a little and let me describe what I was experiencing. Then he said, "I am going to share some Scripture verses with you and if the Holy Spirit is working in your life, they will mean something to you they never have before." He shared Romans 3:23— "For all have sinned and come short of the glory of God." Then, he quoted Romans 6:23—"For the wages of sin is death but the gift of God is eternal life through Jesus Christ our Lord." He took time to explain what these verses meant to me as an individual and that God loved me enough to die for me so I could have eternal life with Him. The final verse he read was Revelation 3:20—"Behold I stand at the door [of your heart] and knock. If any man hear my voice, and open the door, I will come in to him, and will sup with him, and he with me."

The pastor asked me, "Will you open the door of your heart and allow Jesus to come in and take control of your life?" He extended his hand and said, "If so, take my hand and let me lead you in a prayer."

It was difficult to wait until he had finished talking before I said, "Yes, yes, I want Jesus to come into my heart." I grabbed his hand. He led me in prayer as I committed my heart and life to Christ. The peace of God flowed through me and the agitation and frustration I had felt lifted and I knew I would never be the same again.

Our family left to go on vacation later that afternoon. I could not quit sharing with Hugh and the children the wonderful thoughts about what had happened to me. I read Scripture to them and we sang songs all the way to Georgia and Florida. In Savannah, Georgia, we stopped to visit my best friend from elementary and high school. I shared with her and her husband what had happened to me. Several months later she called to tell me she and her husband had become Christians and were attending church regularly.

My hunger and desire to study God's Word increased and I spent every spare minute reading the Bible. My desires changed. I wanted to go to church whereas before, I could take it or leave it. It had not been an important part of my life. My attitude toward people changed. I wanted to reach out and build relationships with others while before, I just wanted to be around one or two friends. All my life I had been plagued by shyness (I would not even talk or pray verbally in a group) and now, little by little, I was willing to take the leadership role, such as becoming president of my Sunday School class. I was also actively involved in other areas of church life. The change in my life was so evident people were asking me what had happened to me. I said, "I committed my heart and life to Jesus, and God has become real to me. He *really* does exist and He *really* does love us." I realized Jesus is absolutely interested in our personal day-by-day lives.

One of the turning points in my life, propelling me to stand before people and teach the Bible, occurred within the year after I became a Christian. My Sunday School teacher was going on vacation for three weeks and asked me to teach the class while she was gone. These ladies were all about my age or a little older. I was scared to death and told her so, but she insisted it would be good for me to do this. So I consented. The studies were in the book of Matthew. I spent many hours studying and found I really enjoyed doing the research. The first Sunday arrived for our forty-five-minute class. I thought I had so much material for the lesson I would not finish, but after twenty minutes I had completed the lesson. I was petrified because we had another twenty minutes to go. Thankfully, people started talking and sharing and we got through the time. The next two Sundays were much better and I found I not only enjoyed preparing the Bible lessons but also presenting them to the class. This was the embryo of the teaching ministry I have been involved with during the years.

The next milestone took place about one and a half years after I became a Christian. My husband is a wonderful man with lots of moral character and integrity, but I realized although he had all these qualities, he too had not had a personal encounter with God. I decided it was my duty to ensure he made this commitment. When he came home for lunch, I would read him Scripture while he ate his peanut butter and jelly sandwich. I had been busy studying the Bible during the morning and did not cook lunch. Luckily, he liked peanut butter and jelly sandwiches!

One day, he walked in for lunch and calmly said, "Claudia, do you think I could have my sandwich without Scripture today please?" How could I refuse such a request asked in such a loving way. He had lunch without Scripture that day and every day after that. When he left to go back to work that day, I just started praying, "Lord, please forgive me for trying to do Your Holy Spirit's work in convicting Hugh of his need for You. I am asking You, Lord, to work in his life in Your own way."

Several weeks later as Hugh and I were talking, he said, "You haven't been reading Scripture to me and nagging me about God. What happened?"

I said, "I found something that works better!" He said, "What's that?" I said, "Prayer." He just got real quiet and did not say anything else. My faith was increased as I learned how to pray for someone else and saw the results. After a time, he began to ask me what I had been studying in the Bible and we would discuss the passages.

A few months later Hugh and I were playing bridge with a couple who were our good friends. Both of them had recently committed their lives to the Lord, so the three of us were talking about what we had been studying in the Bible. Hugh was not entering into the conversation but a little later he said, "Well, I decided I will ask Jesus to take control of my life. I feel like I'm reaching out with one hand and still holding back with the other, but I have seen a change in all of your lives and I want God to work in my life too."

Our lives changed drastically during the years following our commitment to the Lord. It was a result of God changing our hearts as we studied His Word and became involved in the activities of the church. We taught Sunday School, Training Union, home Bible study groups, discipleship studies and went on mission trips with the youth of our church as well as participated in short-term foreign mission trips. All of these activities caused spiritual growth and maturity in our lives. God became important in the decisions we made individually and as a family.

During these years I returned to nursing school. I had taken some classes on and off over the years in hopes of getting a degree someday. The children were all in school and I could attend lectures while they were in classes. After three years, I graduated and passed the state board exams to became a registered nurse. I worked in the local hospitals for some years. It was a good experience but I felt there was something else I should be doing, but at this point I did not have any direction. After six years of nursing, I quit work. Our children were teenagers and I felt the need to be home during those crucial years. We continued our involvement in the church and also participated in family projects.

One of the family projects we did at Christmas for a number of years was to find a family through Social Services who needed help with buying presents and groceries for their children at Christmas. We received a list of items the children wanted for Christmas. Our children, Hope, Bob and April, and I shopped for these items and then wrapped them in appropriate Christmas paper. On Christmas Eve our whole family took all the items we had bought to the family. If the family was receptive, we would share the Christmas story from the Bible with them. We never had anyone turn us down when we asked to share the Bible story. Of course, they could have felt obligated, but we tried not to put any pressure on them to listen if they did not want to. It was a memorable time for all of us. In recent years, we took four of our grandchildren with us when we went to visit our Christmas family. Two of them were old enough to express how much it meant to them.

Our children grew up, went to college and to work. After our youngest daughter went to work, I began to feel it was time to follow through with a nudging I had been feeling for years. The culmination of this desire came about three weeks after my father died. He had been living with us for two and a half years as he was dying with cancer. Before my father's death, my husband and I had signed up for a week-long discipleship seminar at the Baptist retreat center, White

Oak. The seminar was called "MasterBuilder." The church had paid our expenses for this conference. We had debated about canceling since we had just gone through the funeral, but I really felt the different environment would be a good catharsis. Hugh agreed and we went to the conference.

For the week, each person was assigned a group. The leaders put husbands and wives in separate groups. I was in a good group with three Southern Baptist ministers, all male of course. Each group was instructed to share from the heart about things we would like to be or do as Christians.

One question was, "What would you like to be doing in the next five to ten years?" We were to answer that question overnight and come back to the group the next day to discuss it. The group was to comment as to why you could or could not achieve your goal.

I talked it over with my husband that evening because I felt the group I was in would not accept what I really wanted to write down. My husband encouraged me to write it anyway and see what would happen. I wrote, "I would like to obtain a seminary degree and be ordained to the Gospel ministry. I would also like to lead some seminars or women's groups." The next day I went to the group with fear and trepidation. To my complete surprise, this group of Southern Baptist ministers were very supportive, giving me encouragement about why they felt I could accomplish my goals.

We had been together for a week and they offered positive feedback on my gifts that they felt would benefit me in ministry. I felt God gave me His blessing to pursue this desire to go to seminary. When I shared with my husband what had happened, he encouraged me to write to the seminary and get information on admission. I did this and also drove to the seminary for an interview. This was in April 1988 and in June 1988, I was accepted into the seminary for the fall classes. The journey was about to take an unexpected path.

## Reflections on Your Journey

Your circumstances may be different but everyone needs to take time to reflect upon his/her spiritual journey. Please take this opportunity to talk with God and reflect upon your life.

1. When did your journey with God begin?
2. Who or what influenced your journey and growth? Write out the circumstances.
3. What turning points in your life escalated your spiritual growth?
4. Do you feel God is leading you outside your comfort zone in any area of your life? Explain.

*The brightest crowns that are worn in heaven have been tried,*
*and smelted,*
*and polished,*
*and glorified*
*through the furnace of tribulation.*

—Edwin Hubbell Chapin

# Chapter Two

# The Battle Rages

*"...we also rejoice in our sufferings, because we know that suffering produces perseverance; perseverance, character; and character, hope."*

Romans 5:3-4

I arrived at seminary full of excitement and anticipation, which had built to a crescendo for two months after I was accepted. It was the beginning of a new journey in my life. I left home at 4:30 A.M. for the three-and-one-half-hour drive to register for classes and take my belongings to the dorm room and settle in. Students were returning to campus and renewing old acquaintances and making new ones. The atmosphere appeared to be warm and friendly.

While being excited about this new journey in my life, I was nevertheless missing my husband. We had not been separated for any length of time during our married lives. Even though it meant traveling and being away during the week, my husband had agreed that I could follow the call I felt on my life since becoming a Christian at age twenty-five. The Lord has blessed me with a very special husband.

The church I attended for twenty-two years, which actually *birthed* me into the Kingdom of God and nourished and trained me, approved my acceptance into seminary. Everything was wonderful, and fell into place beautifully for me to proceed with the next step of my spiritual journey.

## Controversy on the Campus

These feelings of approval, acceptance and joy were short-lived. A controversy was raging in the seminary I attended. The seminary campus was beautiful, with large oak trees scattered around the majestic old brick buildings. The grass and hedges were neatly trimmed and flowers were planted at various locations around the classroom buildings and library. The birds were singing wonderful melodies. The peace conveyed by the outside surroundings was in direct opposition to the turmoil going on within the hallowed old walls of the buildings. Several issues were involved in the controversy, but one of the major arguments concerned *women in ministry*.

Classrooms became verbal battle grounds. Professors were challenged by fundamentalist students on almost everything they taught. Women were ridiculed if they voiced an opinion about anything. I had the unfortunate and unhappy experience of finding a poem written by one of the fundamentalist men on the copy machine when I tried to make copies of a report I was to turn in at my next class. Here are some excerpts from the poem that will visualize for you some of the battle taking place on campus:

> *So this is a seminary. How can it be? Read these words. Then Judge with me.*
> *Academic freedom? You've got to be kidding. Liberal views are Rampart [sic]. Conservatives are bidding.*
> *"Teach our women to pastor" they blurt and shout. But it's not God's way and they refuse to search it out.*

Written at the bottom of the page was this statement:

> *The customs in some congregations of having a woman as pastor is in flat contradiction to this apostolic teaching and is open rebellion*

*against Christ our King and high treason against His Sovereignty and against nature as well as grace.*

My thought was, "These are the men who will be pastoring churches in the near future?" It was scary. Where was the love and acceptance Jesus taught His disciples to share with others? After reading the poem, and learning it was circulating around the seminary, I sat down and wrote the following letter to the president of the seminary and sent copies to all the professors. Other parts of the previous poem were a direct attack upon the professors, and I wanted them to know not everyone felt what the poem conveyed.

Dear Dr._____,

This week I had the unfortunate and unhappy experience of finding this attached letter on the copy machine in the Library. When I first began to read it my reaction was anger, but then a sadness settled over me. It grieved my heart to realize this man and others like him at _____Seminary will be receiving their degrees in a couple of weeks and will be going out into a world that is desperately in need of love and forgiveness and positive affirmation, to minister. People must have those qualities before they can give them to others. I have seen this man and others of his persuasion verbally attack the professors and women on campus.

When I arrived at _____Seminary last fall, I was somewhat aware of the conflict and controversy but I guess that I still expected (idealistic it may be) to see some koinonia on campus as well as acceptance and respect. I have not found it to be so among the students as a whole and I would have to say, even at my age, I have been disillusioned. This grieves my heart and hinders the work of the Holy Spirit in all of our lives. This lack of koinonia is because of the attitude and spirit of people as revealed by the author of the attached poem. They expect everyone to sign their "doctrinal statement" and if they don't, then they are considered un-Christian or even heretic. All this labeling of Christian brothers and sisters has brought division to the Body of Christ.

The bright spot during these semesters for me has *not* been the student relationships. It has been the professors. I have not met one professor who was a heretic. They have been the epitome of Christian character, which I cannot say for some of the students. When these students have verbally abused or challenged the professors in class, the professors have not retaliated in the same unloving spirit with which they were spoken to. They have spoken in love, understanding and patience, trying to make plain what they said. But those who have their minds already made up just don't have ears to hear anything that differs from their own perspectives. If you don't agree with them, then you are wrong.

The professors I have had the privilege of sitting under have been faithful to their ministry of teaching the subjects that have been entrusted to them. I count it a blessing to have "sat at their feet" and the Lord has used each one to teach me. I have learned from their characters, and their responses, as well as from their lectures. They have handled their subjects with integrity, truth and commitment in the midst of much conflict and frustration. I am grateful to each of them.

I just wanted you to know the poem by_____ does not reflect the attitude of everyone on campus. The _____Seminary catalogue states those who attend_____Seminary are expected to order their lives by Christian standards of character and conduct. That involves more than the letter of the law, "not doing this and that," but it is the Spirit of love, understanding, and forgiveness in the midst of misunderstanding and differences. I don't believe this attached poem reveals an adherence to these standards.

Is this censorious, judgmental spirit what we have to look forward to at _____Seminary? I do believe God desires His people to put away sin, but a "true prophet of God" while judging sin, does it with a tear in his/her heart, in his/her eyes, in his/her voice, and in his/her writing. A true prophet identifies with the people as Isaiah did, "I am a man of unclean lips and dwell in the midst of a people with unclean lips." Let us hear the words of a true prophet, and not the judgmental, unloving "false prophets."

Thank you for allowing me to express my feelings.

Very truly,

Claudia P. Brantley

After receiving this letter, the president of the seminary called me to make an appointment to talk with him, and I did. Several weeks later, I received a letter from the president of the seminary saying he had talked with this man. Several years later, I found out the man who wrote that poem had split the church he was leading and was not pastoring at that time. Perhaps the reason God is calling women to the pulpit ministry is because some men are abdicating their calls of love and compassion toward people.

Suddenly I found myself in a dilemma. My church had approved my entrance into seminary. It never occurred to me that as a woman, my call to be ordained to the *ministerial* ministry would be called into question. My credentials and reputation as a committed lay-servant of God had been proven for more than twenty years in my home church and community. I had been involved in every facet of church life. This included teaching adult Sunday School classes, Bible School, G.A.'s mission organization, teenagers' Training Union groups, helping prepare and going on mission trips to the hills of Kentucky and choir tours into prisons across the country, Women's Missionary Union Bible studies, singing in the choir, being on various committees, (including the nominating committee), and counseling many people. My husband, family and friends were behind me 100 percent, so why all this turmoil, conflict and agony? Foremost in my thoughts was the fact that my denomination really encouraged people to seek and follow God's will, so why all this controversy when someone was trying to do that very thing?

This heated controversy sent me to my Bible to see if God really was against women being ordained to the Gospel ministry or if it was just the narrow-minded view of some people trying to impose their ideas upon other people. Some people tend to use the Bible to restrict the service of women in the church. In doing this, women's self-esteem is crushed and their hearts are wounded. These attitudes cause the church to keep women from being all they can be. This in turn hinders the church from being all it could be. Women may conclude the church has no place for them if they don't fit the established roles for women. Did the Bible really forbid me to become a *she preacher*? I decided to search the Scripture for answers.

# Reflections on Your Journey

Your circumstances may be different but everyone needs to take time to reflect upon his/her spiritual journey. Please take this opportunity to talk with God and reflect upon your life.

1. What is new about your life's journey from when you first began?
2. What obstacles are you facing as you seek to follow God?
3. What Scriptures may be speaking to your situation or experience?
4. Are any persons or organizations opposing you in your goals for your life? Explain.
5. How will you deal with them?

*As sure as ever God puts his children in the furnace,*
*He will be in the furnace with them.*
—Charles Hadden Spurgeon

*Chapter Three*

# Biblical-Historical Background on Women in Ministry

*"The Lord gave the word: the women that publish the tidings are a great host."*
Psalm 68:11 (Hebrew Translation)

*C*ritical biblical interpretation has transformed the study of Scripture during the past century. This has produced different approaches to the study of the Bible. Critical interpretation of the Bible approaches it by seeking to understand the text in light of the times in which it was written. Traditionally the approach to understanding the text was to accept what you read as valid for all times and places. The approach you take in studying the Bible will make a difference in the interpretation of the passages you are seeking to understand. My approach to study of the Bible is to research the times in which the text I am studying was written. I believe this is the best way one can arrive at what God is seeking to say to us in our day and time. That is my approach in the exegetical work that follows.

## Daughters of the Church

Since the noun *prophet* is the word used most often for preachers or ministers of the Gospel, I decided to do a word study. The word *prophet* comes from the Greek *prophetes*. It is from *pro* meaning "*before or for*" and *phemi* meaning "*to speak*." The prophet is thus one who speaks before in the sense of proclaim, or the one who speaks for, i.e. in the Name of God. It is God who invites or impels the prophet(ess) to speak. The prophet(ess) does not force God. God initiates. So a prophet is one who preaches the Gospel and/or speaks for God.

Prophecy in the New Testament included prophetic words given for comfort, encouragement and improvement. The prophetic gift is for the exhortation, edification and instruction of the local churches (I Corinthians 14).

The Old Testament is also filled with examples of *women in ministry*. Isaiah 40:9 translated from literal Hebrew reads, "O woman, that publishest good tidings to Zion, get thee up into the high mountain; O woman, that publishest good tidings to Jerusalem, lift up thy voice with strength; lift it up, be not afraid; say unto the cities of Judah, Behold your God." Psalm 68:11 in the Revised Version is another example of women ministering. It reads, "The Lord giveth the Word: The women that publish the tidings are a great host."

My research led me to find that women are specifically mentioned as prophetesses in the Bible. The Hebrew word for prophet is *nab* and the feminine form for prophetess is *nebiah*. Deborah in Judges 4-5 is probably the most familiar prophetess. She was not only a prophet, but a judge for forty years, and a wife. Barak, the leader of the army would not even go into battle without Deborah being by his side (Judges 4:8). Barak is listed in Hebrews 11:32 as one of the heroes of faith. Deborah was the *only* judge who was also a prophet.

Even if God only mentioned one woman as a prophet, it would be enough to realize God does call women to preach. However, there is even more in the Scriptures about women who were prophets. The Talmud lists four more as prophetesses—Sarah, Hannah, Abigail and Esther. The Israelite's law excluded women from the priesthood but allowed women to be called to the office of prophet.

The Old Testament continues to mention women ministers. Miriam, the prophetess, is mentioned in Exodus 15:20. This passage is called "Miriam's Song." In Numbers 12:1-2 Miriam is numbered among those through whom God spoke, albeit God is chastising Miriam and Aaron because they were speaking against Moses.

Huldah was a prophetess and the wife of Shallum (II Kings 22:14). The priest, Hilkiah (II Chronicles 34:22), and his delegation sought her out to hear what God would say to them. Jeremiah and Zephaniah were prophets in her time, and it is not clear why they were not sought. It could be because she was more accessible in Jerusalem. Huldah pronounced the first official statement of scriptural authority concerning the scroll that was found. Some believe that to be the beginning of the Old Testament canon.

Noadiah was a prophetess mentioned in Nehemiah 6:14. She was included with the prophets who were trying to intimidate Nehemiah.

Isaiah's wife was also a prophetess (Isaiah 8:3). This seems to be the only mention of a prophet and prophetess being married.

The New Testament heralds Anna, the daughter of Phanuel, as a prophetess. She was also married. Anna was old when Jesus was born, and gave praise to God for him (Luke 2:36-37). She declared the redemption that would come through Jesus.

Acts 21:8-10 mentions that Philip the Evangelist had four unmarried daughters. They were also prophetesses.

The Apostle Paul in his writings has revealed women also prophesied. In I Corinthians 11:5, Paul writes, "And every women who prays or prophesies with her head uncovered dishonors her head...." The issue here is not about whether a woman can prophesy. The text shows that she does pray and prophesy in the congregation. Since Paul has made this statement, why would he tell the same women they cannot speak in church and mean they cannot prophesy? Some interpret this passage in I Corinthians 14:33-36 as forbidding women to speak in public gatherings and therefore forbidding them to prophesy. Taken strictly, it would also prevent women from singing congregational hymns.

Some Christians similarly argued against the use of anesthesia in childbirth on the grounds that Genesis 3:16 taught that God's will is that women should suffer and perhaps even die in childbirth. Other Christians have also opposed the whole idea of birth control because God's will for women is motherhood, they say.

In light of this, a different interpretation is needed for these verses. There, the Corinthian church was coming out of a pagan culture. I have been to the ruins of Corinth. The pagan temple to Aphrodite, the goddess of love, is atop the hill near the ruins of the city. At one time, a thousand or more sacred prostitutes served her temple. In pagan worship, it was appropriate and even obligatory for women to shout loudly, moan and babble, while making gyrations with their bodies in a sort of dance. Some of the men and women who were converted in Corinth were coming out of this pagan background and it is possible they were taking their old practices into the Christian churches, disrupting the service. Paul, naturally, told them they must not speak in church in a disruptive way. That makes much more sense than thinking Paul would contradict himself in those two Corinthian passages. If one takes the time to do some in-depth study of the Corinthian church, he/she will find the church had many different problems that Paul had to address.

First Corinthians 11:20-21 mentions one major problem:

> When you come together, it is not the Lord's Supper you eat, for as you eat, each of you goes ahead without waiting for anybody else. One remains hungry, another gets drunk.

They were even getting drunk at the Lord's Supper, but we don't forbid partaking of communion because of the abuses. The Corinthian church was a church with a multitude of problems.

The church in Ephesus, as well as many of the New Testament churches, also had a background of coming out of paganism. Paul could have been addressing specific problems within these churches rather than making a mandate for every church throughout all ages. Perhaps it could be equated to American missionaries entering another culture to present the Gospel. They must deal with the cultural and religious influences of that country within the church.

Let us remember that history does play a part in the interpretation of the Scripture. The explanation of some of the previously mentioned passages has been the cause of women not progressing into leadership positions in the work of the Kingdom of God. For centuries Christian women have been robbed of ecclesiastical status in the Church of Jesus Christ because interpreters of Scripture have failed to perceive the true setting of the Apostle Paul's words. The passages most quoted by the opponents to women in ministry are found in I Corinthians 14:34-35 and I Corinthians 11:5.

We can shine fresh light upon these passages. First Corinthians 14:34 and 35 read in the Revised Standard Version:

> *The women should keep silence in the churches. For they are not permitted to speak, but should be subordinate, as even the law says. If there is anything they desire to know, let them ask their husbands at home. For it is shameful for a woman to speak in church.*

Those who would closely examine the Greek text as well as the historical setting would realize Paul never wrote those words as a *commandment from the Lord*. There were problems in the church at Corinth Paul was addressing and the Judaizers were a major influence. The Judaizers were those Jews who were trying to make the church adhere to Jewish law and customs. One must also remember the earliest Greek manuscripts had no beginning and ending of sentence structure, no capital letters, no commas, no periods, and no quotation marks. Actually, they had no punctuation. The interpreter has to add all these things. Those who read the English Bible are dependent upon the translators for the addition of all these punctuation marks in their translation. Where Paul mentions "not permitted to speak" and "the law says" is not a reference to Scripture but to Jewish tradition and Jewish law. The Jewish Talmud said "it was a shame for a woman to let her voice be heard among men...." There is not a trace from Genesis to Malachi, nor in the *law of Moses* dealing with the subject of women being forbidden to speak. Paul all through the book of Corinthians was addressing the problems the church in Corinth was having, which had been brought to his attention, possibly through a letter they wrote to him that has never surfaced.

The text of I Corinthians 11:2-16 is also open to a different interpretation.

> I commend you because you remember me in everything and maintain the traditions even as I have delivered them to you. But I want you to understand that the head of every man is Christ, the head of a woman is her husband, and the head of Christ is God. Any man who prays or prophesies with his head covered dishonors his head, but any woman who prays or prophesies with her head unveiled dishonors her head—it is the same as if her head were shaven. For if a woman will not veil herself, then she should cut off her hair; but if it is disgraceful for a woman to be shorn or shaven, let her wear a veil. For a man ought not to cover his head, since he is the image and glory of God; but woman is the glory of man
>
> I Corinthians 11:2-7 RSV

The veil was called a *tallith*. The Jewish Christians wore veiling according to the *custom* of the Jews. Veiling was a sign of reverence before God and a condemnation for sin to the Jews. The Christian church consisted largely of Roman converts, and the Romans also veiled. The question then arose in Corinth whether the Christian women as well as the Christian men should veil. According to the oral law of the Jews, the married man (*aner*) was commanded to wear the *tallith*.

Since the *tallith* was a sign of guilt and condemnation, when a Christian covered his head with it, he was acknowledging guilt and condemnation. It was a dishonor to his head, Christ, who had made atonement for his sins. "There is now no condemnation to those who are in Christ Jesus" (Romans 8:1). Paul is saying if the wife in unveiling her head would bring dishonor or shame to her husband, *then let her be veiled* when she prays or prophesies, since it is the Jewish custom. Paul is stating here that women do pray or prophesy in the church but after the oral tradition she should let her head be covered when she does, so she does not disgrace her husband. According to the Jewish custom of that time, oral law made it so disgraceful a thing that Christian women would find it difficult to put away the veil, but

Paul is not making it a mandate for the church. He is again addressing a problem within the church at Corinth.

Today if women were to walk into a Christian church in America wearing a veil, they would be out of place and people would stare at them. In New Testament times, if the women had not worn veils they would have been out of place.

The third passage those who want to deny ordination to women have misinterpreted is found in I Timothy 2:8-15, and was written approximately ten years after the letter to the Corinthians.

> *I desire then that in every place the men should pray, lifting holy hands without anger or quarreling; also that women should adorn themselves modestly and sensibly in seemly apparel, not with braided hair or gold or pearls or costly attire but by good deeds, as befits women who profess religion. Let a woman learn in silence with all submissiveness. I permit no woman to teach or to have authority over men; she is to keep silent. For Adam was formed first, then Eve; and Adam was deceived, but the woman was deceived and became a transgressor. Yet woman will be saved through bearing children, if she continues in faith and love and holiness with modesty*
>
> I Timothy 2:8-15 RSV

This epistle is written to address administration problems within the church and to oppose false teaching.

Rabbinical teaching gradually began to infiltrate the Christian church in the early centuries of Christianity regarding the roles of women. This colored Christian theology regarding women the world over. One of the most serious mistranslations in our English version of the Bible is the root for misinterpretation of some of Paul's writings.

Translators use Genesis 3:16 to interpret Paul's words in I Corinthians 11:3 and I Timothy 2:11. Genesis 3:16 in the Revised Version reads: "Unto the woman, he said, I will greatly multiply thy sorrow and thy conception; in sorrow thou shalt bring forth children and thy desire shall be to thy husband and he shall rule over thee."

In the RV, *desire* has been grievously translated, changing the whole meaning of the passage. The original word is *teshuqa* and is used only three times in the Old Testament; Genesis 3:16; 4:7 and Song of Solomon 7:10. The word *teshuqa* has been rendered *turning* in every version up to one hundred years after Christ. This included the Septuagint Greek, the Syriac Peshito, the Samaritan and Old Latin, which all rendered the word as *turning*. God said Eve was *turning* to Adam (Genesis 3:16) that Abel was *turning* to Cain (Genesis 4:7) and that Christ is *turning* toward his bride (Song of Solomon 7:10), the church. That is one interpretation of who this passage refers to.

The word translated *conception* in the RV was translated in the Septuagint Greek, the oldest translation, as the word *sighing*. Genesis 3:16 should read: "Unto the woman he said, a snare hath increased thy sorrow and thy *sighing*; in sorrow shall thou bring forth children; thou art *turning* to thy husband and he will rule over thee." This passage does not contain a *law* of preordained subordination of woman as is suggested by its use in the New Testament margins of many translations.

Eve went forth from Eden not *cursed* but a forgiven and restored believer. You may ask, "How can one say Eve is a believer?" In Genesis 4:1, Eve says, "I have gotten a man—even the Coming One." She had faith. Eve believed God and His promise of a Savior.

In deeper study of the Scripture in Genesis concerning Adam and Eve, it is found that Eve was deceived by Satan but Adam willfully sinned. He was not beguiled by the serpent. Adam knew what God said about eating of the tree and he ate anyway: God said, "Have you eaten of the tree of which I told you not to eat?" (Genesis 3:11). Adam willfully ate, whereas the serpent beguiled Eve. There is a difference. Also God banished Adam from the Garden of Eden ("God sent forth man from the Garden of Eden and placed the cherubim, and a flaming sword which turned every way, to guard the way to the tree of life" Genesis 3:24). God did not command Eve to leave, but she *turned* to Adam and went with him.

During the time between the Old and New Testaments, the Jews tried to reconcile Jewish customs and the teachings of the Old Testament with Greek paganism. When Christianity came along, they tried to reconcile the Jewish customs and laws with the teachings of Christianity.

Paul gets bad press concerning his attitude toward women. The teaching that God punishes women for the sin of Eve is a wicked and cruel superstition and unworthy of intelligent Christians. It has also created in women a lack of self-respect and self-confidence and limited their spiritual activity. This in turn causes the whole church of Jesus Christ to suffer spiritual and moral loss.

Misinterpretation has caused much division and pain within the Christian church regarding the ordination of women. After all, on the day of Pentecost, the beginning of the Christian church, the Holy Spirit fell on both women and men (Acts 2:17-18). The passage in I Corinthians 12:8-11 reveals the gifts of the Holy Spirit are not given based on gender. It is the Spirit who gives the gifts.

The Apostle Paul was surrounded by women coworkers. Romans 16 mentions people ministering with Paul and almost one-half of them were women. It seems in Romans 16:7 a woman named Junius was an apostle. This was accepted until about the thirteenth century when some theologians tried to introduce Junia as a substitute for Junius.

Paul characterizes the women he lists, Phoebe, Priscilla, Mary, Tryphena, Tryphosa, Julia, Nereus' sister, in the same terms as his male coworkers—Timothy, Apollos, Epaphras, Titus. The verb "work very hard" in Romans 16:6, 12 is often used of *ministerial service*.

Phoebe is called a deacon and one who presides. Paul did not even distinguish gender by calling Phoebe a deaconess but rather a deacon. Paul said she is a *prostatis*. The literal meaning of this word is "one who stands before." It is the noun form corresponding to the verb translated *rule* in I Timothy 3:4, 5, 12 and 5:17. The word in Greek means "a leader, a chief, a protector or a champion."

Women deacons are mentioned in Romans 16:1-2 and I Timothy 3:11. In I Timothy 3:11 some have interpreted this to mean wives of the deacons but the correct translation is the women likewise must be worthy of respect. The word translated *deacon* (I Timothy 4:6, Colossians 1:7, Ephesians 6:21 RSV) is understood to mean "minister." The ordination service of deaconesses is still preserved in the *Apostolic Constitutions*

(VIII.19-20). Early paintings in the catacombs show women in an authoritative position of a bishop, conferring blessings on Christians of both sexes. Two frescos appear to show women serving communion. Tertullian, one of the earliest of the Latin fathers, notes that women appear in every *early* reference to ecclesiastical orders.

Priscilla worked right along side her husband in Romans 16:3-4, Acts 18:18-19, 26, I Corinthians 16:19 and II Timothy 4:19. Priscilla's name is usually mentioned first, which is significant in Jewish writings. The more important person was usually mentioned first.

Paul in Galatians 3:28 declares that "in Christ there is neither Jew nor Greek, slave nor free, *male or female* [italics added], for you all are one in Christ Jesus." Christians, male and female, are represented as "living stones—built into a spiritual house to be a holy priesthood, offering spiritual sacrifices acceptable to God through Jesus Christ" (I Peter 2:5). In respect to our position in Christ, the New Testament obliterates any distinction of rank between male and female.

Prohibitions were issued against women's ministerial activities beginning around A.D. 350. Some of these activities included:

—presiding over churches and serving as priests
—baptizing
—ordination of deaconesses
—establishing presbyteries
—approaching the altar.

These prohibitions indicate the previous existence of these offices for women.

Next, we must look at Jesus' attitude toward women. Jesus lifted women to a higher level of appreciation than they had ever experienced. His position toward women opened up new avenues of ministry for women within the early church.

Mary, the mother of Jesus, was one of the worshipers in the upper room (Acts 1:14). Women as well as men could be baptized (Acts 8:12; 16:15). Women could perform the ministry of prophesying (Acts 2:18; 21:19, I Corinthians 11:5). Jesus' ministry of healing was given to females and males (Luke 13:10-17). Jesus allowed the women to speak directly to Him ( John 4) whereas Jewish rabbis were not permitted to even speak to a woman. Women were followers of Jesus and He encouraged it (Luke 8:2-5). After the resurrection, Jesus appeared first to the women. The women were the bearers of the good news even to His disciples. The disciples first heard the news of Jesus' resurrection from the women (Matthew 28:8-10, Mark 16:1-12, Luke 24:1-12 and John 20:14-16).

Mary Magdalene is really the first one to proclaim the sermon of the resurrection to the disciples. "He is risen" was her message. So it can truthfully be said, a woman is the first preacher to deliver the Gospel message after the death and resurrection of Jesus ( John 20:10-18). Jesus gave her a mandate to deliver the message of His resurrection to the disciples.

The Bible seems to make ambiguous statements regarding matters of female clergy. Some passages seem to imply clearly a commitment to gender inequality (I Timothy 2:11-12, I Corinthians 14:33b-35) while others seem to imply a commitment to gender equality (Galatians 3:28, I Corinthians 11:4-5, Acts 2:16-18, Galatians 5:1). This reveals that other interpretations are a possibility. There are no dogmatic rules concerning women clergy in the Scripture but early church history supports women as clergy. Dorothy Irvin, in *The Ministry of Women in the Early Church: The Archaeological Evidence, Duke Divinity School Review*, no. 2, (1980:76-78) wrote:

> In a Roman basilica dedicated to two women saints, Prudentiana and Praxedis, there is a mosaic. It portrays four figures: the above two saints, Mary and a fourth woman who is unrecognizable. The others are easily recognizable. The face on the far left is identified as Theodora Episcopa, which means Bishop Theodora.
>
> The masculine form for bishop in Latin is episcopus and the feminine form is episcopa. The physical and grammatical evidence proves unmistakably that Bishop Theodora was a woman. The a on Theodora has been partially effaced by scratches across the glass tiles of the mosaic, leading to the disturbing conclusion that attempts were made to deface the feminine ending, perhaps even in antiquity.

An honest student of the Scripture should have no doubt that women figured prominently in Jesus' life and ministry, both during His lifetime and after His resurrection when the first communities were formed and His message began to spread. If these accounts of women's important participation had not been grounded in intractable fact, they would not have survived in such a male-dominated culture. But because such independence and prominence on the part of women conflicted directly with the view of women's roles that pervaded Greco-Roman society, these traditions were ignored and submerged as much as possible in order to conform Christian teaching and practice to social convention. Yet, women were still recognized in the Bible for their leadership in the early church.

The scriptural interpretation I have presented would not have been acceptable to a large group of men at the seminary I was attending. Their minds were made up and all who did not agree with them were heretics. The battle was raging in the hallowed halls and on the grounds of this once tranquil institute of religious training.

The seminary was not the only battlefield. My home church was coming into the war. The battle was beginning to escalate to proportions of deep treachery.

## Reflections on Your Journey

Your circumstances may be different but everyone needs to take time to reflect upon his/her spiritual journey. Please take this opportunity to talk with God and reflect upon your life.

1. Do you feel your method of studying the Bible is adequate for you? Why or why not?
2. Would you be interested in changing the way you study your Bible?
3. If yes, would you consider trying the inductive Bible study method as briefly explained below?
   A. Read the passage you are studying in its context, taking note of who is the writer, the speaker and the recipient.
   B. What is the author's purpose for writing the book and/or passage?
   C. Use a concordance to look up cross references.
   D. Do word studies of key words using Vine's or Strong's Concordance.
   E. Ask the five W and H questions: who, what, when, why, where and how.
   F. Personalize the Scripture for your life.
   G. Research life during the times in which the Scripture was written.

4. Write out how the study of God's Word has changed your life.
5. What new insights have you gained from reading this chapter?

*"You will never learn faith in easy circumstances.*
*When God stretches you, you never snap back to your original shape."*
John L. Mason, author of *You're Born An Original, Don't Die a Copy*

*Chapter Four*

# High Treason

*"No weapon formed against you will prevail, and you will refute every tongue that accuses you. This is the heritage of the servants of the Lord, and this is their vindication from me," saith the Lord.*

Isaiah 54:17

When I went to seminary, my home church pastor said he would ordain me. Now, a year into seminary, I was being told I could not be ordained in my denomination, in my home church.

After attending seminary for about a year, I could see the handwriting on the wall. The seminary continued to be a hotbed of controversy, escalating in intensity. The Southern Baptist Convention was getting more and more adamant and militant about the ordination of women. So I wrote and asked my pastor if I could be ordained before the controversy escalated further. After all, he had told me, and my husband, that he would ordain me. In Southern Baptist churches, one does not have to have a seminary degree or even a college degree to be ordained. I expected to talk with him while I was at home over the weekend.

## Betrayal Personified

Sunday morning at church, the pastor asked me and my husband to come to his study that evening to discuss ordination. We thought he was going to go over plans for my ordination. When we arrived at the pastor's study after the evening church service, he had another staff member and a deacon with him. The discussion did not proceed as my husband and I thought it would. The pastor proceeded to tell me that he would *not* ordain me at the church.

I was totally stunned and after remaining silent for a long moment, I asked him, "Why won't you ordain me? Do you feel I'm not called by God?"

He said, "No, that isn't it at all. I know God's hand is on you. The problem is mine, not yours. I'm concerned about what my conservative friends in the Southern Baptist Convention will say if I ordain you."

You have probably remembered my denomination *was* Southern Baptist. Southern Baptists had begun ordaining a few women in 1964 and the trend had continued through the seventies and early eighties without too much repercussion. Each Southern Baptist church had been free to decide for itself whether or not to ordain women in the absence of a denominational policy. Now the battle was raging and the Southern Baptist Convention (SBC) was trying to set policy that would make churches feel they could not ordain women. Technically, Southern Baptist churches are reputed to be autonomous, meaning they do not have to abide by the SBC if they choose not to. Each church, supposedly, is free to make its own choices.

One deacon, actually a kind man, said I could be ordained in a church in a nearby city that was more *liberal* about the ordination of women. Another leader in the church also said, "Claudia, you cannot be ordained in this church because of what the 'conservative group' in the SBC would think about our church."

My response to the pastor's comment that Sunday evening was, "That reason is not good enough. I won't be held back from doing what I feel God wants me to do because of other people's narrow-mindedness and prejudice."

He tried to appease me by saying the church would give me a "license to the Gospel ministry, and make a big to-do about it at an evening service." Licenses are given in the Baptist denomination to the young men and sometimes women, who need to be proved and are going to seminary.

I said "No, I'm older and my life has already been proven right here at this church." The tears streamed down my face as I spoke and my heart was heavy. Of course, it became a battle that produced in me feelings of rejection and hurt. My heart was burdened and I felt rejection and hurt because my denomination and church leaders were not honoring their commitment. After all, they had voted that it was okay for me to go to seminary and get a Master of Divinity degree. Now I was being told I could not be ordained in my church. I felt totally betrayed and I thought, "This is high treason."

On my drive home I cried copious tears. After a few days, other feelings also surfaced, such as self-doubt, insecurity, anger and loneliness. My thinking became distorted, "If my denomination wasn't willing to ordain me then I must not be worthy to be ordained." That is how self-doubt and insecurity raised their ugly heads. The pain seemed unbearable.

Then after feeling sorry for myself because of the self-doubt and insecurity, I got angry. "Who are 'they' to tell me God isn't calling me to be an ordained minister?" I thought. How would I deal with all these overwhelming emotions that eventually sent me into such a terrible time of disillusionment, discouragement and depression? One of the definitions of depression often expressed is, "Depression is anger turned inward." That is exactly what happened to me.

It would be great if I could say I shook off all those terrible feelings immediately or that I had a wonderful attitude and all my anger and depression vanished and joy overflowed in my life. However, that would be untrue. I cried many, many tears over the next few years. I began an unexpected journey and what a journey! It took me five years to arrive at the destination of joy and peace once again.

The insecurity and lowered-self esteem caused me to withdraw in many ways. I didn't want to go to the worship service at my home church. Now that was a fine attitude for a ministerial student. I did

continue to go to Sunday School. My husband and I had been teaching a couples class for years.

I had always taken the initiative to make luncheon or shopping
appointments with friends, but I stayed home more frequently and did
not make calls. When friends called I did not want to talk. Even though
I continued my seminary training, I questioned my call into the ministry. To be really honest, I must confess, I was mad at God. My reason-
ing was, "God, I have been faithful to Your call on my life and You don't
seem to be doing Your part. Why is all this happening?" (Now don't be
shocked. If you are honest, I bet you have been mad at God, too.)

In Christian churches sometimes, we are not willing to admit we
have negative emotions with which we must deal. People tend to put
on their *spiritual* faces and pretend everything is going great when
they are really dealing with terrible feelings and situations. I found in
my life as a Christian that it is best to be honest before God about my
feelings and situations. After all, God knows them anyway. The faster
we confess our weaknesses, the quicker they can be dealt with in our
lives. So honesty is the best policy in our relationship with God as
well as with other people.

The battle also continued to rage at seminary. The controversy
there began to take on deeper and deeper chasms of separation
among the students. Some students tried to force other students to
take a stand for *their side*. One big word in the controversy was the
*inerrancy* of the Bible. The choices were *liberal* or *conservative*. You were
liberal if you refused to use the word *inerrant* in describing the Bible
and you were conservative if you said the Bible was inerrant. Using
just the word *infallible* was not good enough. I decided to use the old
standard dictionary to look up the words *inerrant* and *infallible*. I
found *inerrant* meant "making no mistakes." It was an absolute word.
*Infallible* meant "incapable of error in setting forth doctrine on faith
and morals." Since there are no original manuscripts of the Bible, and
the copies do have grammatical errors in them, I did not feel the word
*inerrant* to describe the Bible was appropriate, since it means
absolutely without errors. To me the Bible is without error in setting
forth doctrine on faith and morals. I believed that using the word
*infallible* was enough in describing the Bible. An earlier copy of *The*

*Baptist Faith and Message,* a booklet on Baptist doctrine, put out by the Southern Baptist Convention, used the word *infallible* to describe the Bible and not *inerrant.* To be conservative, which meant using *inerrant* to describe the Bible, was acceptable and to be liberal, not using the word *inerrant* to describe the Bible, was not. There could be no middle road or you were ostracized. The conservatives, taking a literal translation and not studying the times in which the Bible was written, were against the ordination of women. Simply put, to be conservative meant you were *against women in ordained ministry.* To be liberal meant you were *for women in ordained ministry.* The tensions mounted. The campus was alive with the sound of arguments in the classrooms, in the dorms and on the campus grounds.

High treason loomed even larger when the Southern Baptist Convention began to circulate the resolution made against women in ministry. In part it read:

> *Whereas, while Paul commends women and men alike in other roles of ministry and service (Titus 2:1-10), he excludes women from pastoral leadership (I Timothy 2:12) to preserve a submission God requires because the man was first in creation and the woman was first in the Edenic fall (I Timothy 2:13).*

The resolution ended with:

> *Therefore, be it resolved…that we encourage the service of women in all aspects of church life and work other than pastoral functions and leadership roles entailing ordination.*

Churches refusing to ordain women as pastors, elders, and deacons place limitations upon God. The Scripture affirms that God is no respecter of persons (Acts 10:34). Women and men equally reflect the image of God. "So God created man in his own image, in the image of God he created him; male and female he created them" (Genesis 1:27). God also has maternal attributes (Psalm 131:2; Isaiah. 42:14). The Scripture testifies God is male and female because male and female are made in His image (Genesis 1:27).

Churches which exclude women from participating in spiritual leadership also limit the image of God. In addition, they place restrictions upon the call of God and on the gifts of the Holy Spirit. To deny the gifts of pastor, elder or deacon to women is to deny the action and teaching of Christ.

Perhaps some of the reasons some men refuse to recognize women as ministers are:

—Men stereotype women into the traditional roles of wife, mother, homemaker, etc.

—Men view women pastors as feminists.

—Men consider women to be too emotional.

—Men resent women in leadership roles.

—Men refuse to accept that women have just as much capability to serve as pastors as they do.

—Men hold on to the *traditions of men* rather than seeking out truth for themselves from the Word of God.

People who refuse to accept women as ministers have not considered the unarguable reason for women to be chosen as ministers. It is the doctrine of the *priesthood of all believers*. The Baptists, as well as other denominations, tenaciously give credence to this doctrine. Yet women are being denied the right to follow the call God has on their lives. They feel betrayed by the denominations that birthed and nourished them.

Finally, one day I had had enough. No, I was not going to give up on God or quit seminary, but I decided it was time to transfer to a different seminary with an environment conducive to Christian principles and biblical truths in order to continue my spiritual journey.

# Reflections on Your Journey

⮜✦⮞

Your circumstances may be different but everyone needs to take time to reflect upon his/her spiritual journey. Please take this opportunity to talk with God and reflect upon your life.

1. Is there anybody or anything in your life you feel has betrayed you in some way?
2. How did he/she/it make you feel?
3. What was your initial response to the situation?
4. What were subsequent responses to the situation?
5. What did you learn through these experiences? Explain.

*"You don't measure the success of a person by the level of position they obtain, but by the number of obstacles they overcome."*

—Booker T. Washington

*Chapter Five*

# Breaking the Barriers

*"He heals the brokenhearted and binds up their wounds."*

Psalm 147:3

During my Thanksgiving break while at home, I made an appointment with the Dean at a seminary of a different denomination. I was very impressed with what I heard and saw, and I submitted my application.

After one and a half years at the Southern Baptist Seminary, I transferred to a Presbyterian Seminary closer to home. This seminary had not been affected by the controversy of *women in ministry* even though it too was operated by a denomination that did not believe in ordaining women. The difference was in the attitudes of the leadership and students in the seminary. People were allowed to be themselves and follow the lead of God even if it differed from the denominational philosophy. This was especially true for women from other denominations. This move proved to be a most positive experience. People could discuss topics and even disagree and still be friends with one another. What a joy it was! The professors were very supportive of my call to the ministry. Their influence helped bring acceptance and healing back into areas of my life which were badly wounded. I still had a long way to go but once again I could see the hand of God on my life guiding me. It was time to break the barriers hindering me from reaching the levels of ministry I felt God was calling me to.

I also received affirmation from family, friends and seminary colleagues that I was doing just what God wanted me to do. I still have many letters and notes from friends and family who wrote me words of encouragement during my seminary years. Often those notes and letters would arrive at a time when discouragement was at its worst. They were like little smiles and pats on the back from God saying, "I care and I am here for you, just keep your eyes on Me."

After attending the Presbyterian Seminary for another one and a half years, I graduated with a Master of Divinity degree, with honors. My Sunday School teacher who had encouraged me to teach her Sunday School class in my early Christian walk wrote me a note upon my graduation from seminary. She said:

> "I admire you greatly for your determined perseverance. Surely, God is preparing you for a distinctive service in His Kingdom."

This *distinctive service* God had for me in His Kingdom was not in evidence. Now the question was, "What is the next step on this spiritual journey God had set before me?" It was a good thing I did have *determined perseverance*. Even though I had changed seminaries, I was still attending my home church in a denomination that did not want to ordain women. What was the next step of this journey?

I did not feel I should give up the battle, although I was sorely tempted at times. Once again I wrote a letter to the pastor of my home church, asking that the Board of Deacons and congregation vote on my being ordained. This time, he consented to bring my request to the Board for a vote. My husband was on the Board of Deacons at the time and had been for many years. He said it was the first time in all his years on the Deacon Board they had taken a secret ballot. My husband also told me the comments the deacons made during the discussion were all very positive about my life. The vote was in my favor from the deacons, although I found out through someone who helped count the votes that it was not unanimous. He said, "An overwhelming majority voted for you and you can feel very supported by your church." When the vote went before the congregation, there was no negative discussion and no dissenting vote. This vote was by a show of hands. The pastor wrote me a letter telling me the deacons and congregation had voted in favor of my ordination and informed me he had asked our associate pastor to oversee my ordination. I had previously been told, "Claudia, if you pursue ordination here, it will split the church." God is faithful and in March 1991, I was ordained to the Gospel Ministry at my home church, which was in a denomination that did not believe women should be ordained. The pastor left town after the morning service on the day of my ordination to speak in another town and did not participate in my ordination service. That too was a deep hurt, but I saw God move in spite of opposition and the church did not split; in fact, there was not even a ripple.

The only ripples were in my heart. All this emotional trauma took a tremendous toll on me. I felt so rejected and suffering seemed to be a permanent part of my life. While men are encouraged and supported in their decision for the ministry, women get an unenthusiastic response. I was never asked to preach a sermon in my home church where I had been a member for twenty-five years, and that was very painful. For many months, every time I walked into my home church, I choked up and tears welled up in my eyes. It takes a strong sense of calling to overcome the barriers that are raised against women going into the ministry. It was the grace of God that saw me through and enabled me to continue my journey.

## A Dilemma

A dilemma still existed. There were no opportunities in the area we lived in for me to become a pastor or associate pastor of a Southern Baptist church. The few churches in our area open to women ministers already had women on staff. My husband is a banker and had been at the same place over twenty-five years. He was not changing jobs, we were not moving from our home, and we were not separating. Since we were not moving just so I could have a place of service, the question I asked God was, "What is the next step? Where is the path upon which I am to continue my ministerial journey?"

Suffice it to say, the next part of the journey was not pleasant either, but by this time I had realized God was trying to teach me some things. I began to see I was not trusting God with my situation. Being the resourceful person I am, I was trying to work things out in my own mind and strength. *Waiting* was not part of my spiritual vocabulary. My philosophy was *doing anything* was better than *doing nothing*. I learned that waiting on God can be a spiritual exercise of faith.

Another lesson I learned was, God is more interested in our character than He is in our comfort. God is much more interested in building faithfulness, fortitude, discipline and moral strength into our lives than making us comfortable. I certainly was not comfortable during the next one and a half years, but I continued to learn how to know Him and His ways through the painful circumstances of life. Often, pain and discouragement draw us into the presence of God as nothing else does. In His presence we see ourselves as He sees us and it is not always pleasant. I began to see that anger led to unforgiveness and hostility toward those I felt had thwarted me. This was not the character God wanted to see in His children.

Gradually, I began to realize I needed to forgive those people who had injured me emotionally. God had forgiven me for everything I had ever done that displeased Him, and I needed to forgive those whom I felt had caused me pain and suffering. I came to this realization kicking and fussing. My argument with God was, "They are the ones in the wrong. They are the ones who need to ask forgiveness. Why do I have to forgive them?"

Because "I forgive those who forgive others." That is what God's Word said to me (Matthew 6:14). Just uttering the words "I forgive" was not enough. I had to take positive steps to show forgiveness. I did this through maintaining a relationship with people from whom I really wanted to pull away. This was a process in my life which reaped results over a period of time. I did not isolate myself from those who were disagreeing with me over the ordination of women. My Heavenly Father gave me love and forgiveness toward those whom I felt had put obstacles in my life as I persevered.

Behind every cloud there is a silver lining, or so I had heard. I was not recognizing the silver lining yet. At this point my cloud happened to be a non-denominational church where I was an associate pastor for one and a half years. This opportunity arose because of friends who were part of this church, who knew I needed a place of ministry and who felt I could help people grow in the area of discipleship. It also seemed to be the only place open for me to minister at this point. To complete my doctoral dissertation project, I also needed a place of service. The leaders of the non-denominational church had told my husband and me they were open to *women in ministry* when I interviewed for the position. Mark Chaves in his book *Ordaining Women-Culture and Conflict in Religious Organizations* (page 2, Harvard University Press, Cambridge, Massachusetts-1997) says, "Some denominations give verbal assent that they are fully supportive of gender equality even as they formally deny women access to key leadership positions."

It did not take me long to realize the pastors had given verbal assent to women ministers but their actions belied their statement. I found I was in a very mismatched situation, to say the least. The co-pastors did not want other ideas presented to them that differed from their ideas, especially from a woman, although they would never admit it.

One day I walked into the workroom where the copy machine was located. When I opened it to copy something, there was a paper on *Why Women Should Not Be Elders*. (I am very cautious now when I raise the top of a copy machine. I found it can lead me into conflicts I had rather avoid.) I took the paper to the co-pastors who were in the office with the door closed. They would often meet and leave me out of the loop. I handed them the paper and told them, "If you are considering not having women elders, it seems like a contradiction to have a woman pastor on staff. If you decide to make that change, let me know and I will have to resign." I then left the office, gently closing the door, because I really felt like slamming it shut.

There were more than several discussions involving differing ideas. Someone in the church once said to me, "If you disagree with the pastors, you will be on their blacklist." This proved to be a true statement. I feel people should be free to express their ideas even if they differ from one another, as long as it is done respectfully.

My doctoral committee at seminary, being aware of the situation, told me I should leave before the situation worsened. I thought, "There are people in this church who really want to grow spiritually and I can help them." I also needed a place of ministry for my doctoral project, and I did not have anywhere else to minister in our area. So I stayed even though it was an uncomfortable situation and potentially volatile.

The tensions increased and it was more than obvious that the pastors did not want to hear any ideas differing from their own. One morning shortly after arriving at work, I was called into the office. The co-pastors told me, "You aren't being submissive to our authority so we are going to fire you." They did fire me and refused to let me resign because as they stated, "We want to teach you to be submissive to authority." It was a blessing in disguise (I realized later), but at that time it was another very painful experience, coming on the heels of all the pain and suffering and rejection I had been through concerning my ordination. My depression escalated. For weeks, I slept for hours during the day and I had never even been a nap person. I could not even pray. "Where are you, God?" was the only utterance I made to the heavens.

My silver lining emerged, and it was seminary. My work on a Doctor of Ministry degree slowed down considerably and it took me an extra year to complete my doctoral project. I had to find another place to do my research project because I needed a group to work with. My project was entitled *Equipping the Saints: Training People in the Church to Lead Inductive Bible Studies,* and involved just what the title suggested. Ironically, I was able to have participants from my home church in which I was ordained take part in the doctoral study group. The new Minister of Education was eager to help and supported me.

This proved to be a time of some healing and growing because of my contact with students and professors at the seminary. The doctoral committee was also so supportive and accepting of me and my ministry. God gave me glimpses of Himself through people He placed in my life.

## Emotions, Emotions, Emotions

During the time immediately after I graduated from seminary, having received my Doctor of Ministry degree, I experienced severe depression. It caused me to withdraw from involvement in almost everything except what I just had to do. The black hole of depression left feelings of hopelessness I cannot explain to one who has not had that experience. Since I had worked as a registered nurse (R.N.) and studied psychiatric nursing, I recognized my symptoms of depression: a loss of interest in life, crying at the drop of a hat, headaches and a slowing down because of lack of energy, which was unusual for me. Then I had a change in eating habits that led to weight gain. Some people lose weight when they are depressed but wouldn't you just know, I wasn't one of those people. Discouragement is often the fruit of depression. Since it seemed I was destined to remain in that state, I lost my desire and love of life. Every day was drudgery. I had no female mentors to share my experiences with, and the silences of God were very loud.

Depression is one of the most significant consequences of refusing to forgive the people who have wronged us. Emotional energy is required to maintain a grudge so our emotional energy is exhausted as well as physical energy. The degree our thoughts are off the mark of the way God thinks will be the same degree we suffer emotionally. Feelings come from thoughts, either conscious or subconscious. If we allow the Holy Spirit to change our thoughts, we can have our emotions changed. If our values change, our actions change. This was a slow process for me, perhaps because of stubbornness. This deep depression prevailed for almost two years, but I learned a lot during that time. A root of bitterness can grow out of the soil of depression. Perhaps when Jesus said, "Forgive seventy times seventy," He was keenly aware of the mental, physical, emotional and spiritual consequences of holding on to resentments. Medical experts today talk about the physical consequences of anger and bitterness. These negative emotions can produce stress on the body leading to colitis, high blood pressure, ulcers and arthritis, to name a few things. The Scriptures suggest frequently that negative thinking can be "rottenness of the bones, but a heart at peace gives life to the body" (Proverbs 14:30). My physical symptoms came out in the area of my thyroid, resulting in hypothyroidism. Depression can be a major symptom of hypothyroidism. This went undiagnosed for two years, which led to deeper depression.

My heart was not at peace. The only thing I could do at this point was to keep on keeping on, doing the routine things of everyday life. People I had developed relationships with over the years still sought me out to counsel them with their problems. Thinking of other people's needs also gave me some relief. It helped me take the focus off myself.

One thing I learned about myself was when I felt out of control and could see no way out, I became depressed. That had never happened to me before. This is especially true when I tried to work things out, and left God out of my decision-making processes. God taught me that He always provides what I need (not necessarily what I want) if I will turn to Him. This was a process, as most learning situations are in our lives.

Another insight I gleaned through my experiences was how I had allowed other people's opinions or perceived opinions and the circumstances in my life to influence my view of myself. This led to my self-image being adversely affected, which decreased my productivity and creativity.

Thanks be to God, gradually I began to come back to the land of the living. The Lord used the love, loyalty and prayers of my husband, my family and my friends. (I have been free of depression for eight years, and I never want to experience anything like that again.) Even in the midst of that time, I realize God's hand was upon my life. He was with me. God used the obstacles and experiences in my life to teach me so much. I have more compassion and patience for those who experience things out of their control. God truly knows what I need to build His character in my life. He increased my faith in Him as my source. He showed me He is always there, and always in control. God can break the barriers in our lives.

Even after the barrier of depression was broken, I found I still had no sense of direction regarding ministry. The difference now was I had peace about the situation. I still attended a church in the denomination in which I had been ordained, but the doors of the *ministerial* ministry were closed in the denomination that had birthed me.

*Character cannot be developed in ease and quiet.*
*Only through experiences of trial and suffering can the soul be*
*strengthened, vision cleared, ambition inspired and success achieved.*
—Helen Keller

## Reflections on Your Journey

Your circumstances may be different but everyone needs to take time to reflect upon his/her spiritual journey. Please take this opportunity to talk with God and reflect upon your life.

1. What can you do to break the negative cycles in your life?
2. What barriers need to be broken for you to move on with God in your spiritual life?
3. Have you struggled with the "silences of God?" Explain.
4. Do you have any roots of bitterness in your life? Name them.
5. What opportunities might you have missed in seeing God's hand in your circumstances?
6. What did you learn about God in dealing with the obstacles in your life?

*No wound? No scar?*
*Yet as the Master shall thy servant be*
*And pierced are the feet that follow Me:*
*But thine are whole.*
*Can he have followed far*
*Who has not wound nor scar?*

—Amy Carmichael, *Thou Givest…They Gather*
(Fort Washington, PA: *Christian Literature Crusade*, 1958, Page 90).

# Chapter Six

# Beyond Grief and Anger

*"If I regard iniquity in my heart the Lord will not hear me."*

Psalm 66:18

Part of my ministerial journey took me back into the hospital setting. I had left the hospital behind seven years before when I gave up my nursing career. One of the requirements in my seminary training was to take Clinical Pastoral Education (CPE). I chose to do this at our local regional medical center so I could remain at home for the summer. It is a program that requires a lot of time and energy. As clergy, we take care of the spiritual needs of patients going through traumatic emotional and physical experiences while in the hospital. Part of the training involved intensive interaction among all the clergy participating in the program. It is a great program that all pastors should consider experiencing. It enhances the pastor's ministry and makes him/her more sensitive to the experiences and needs of other people. It also brings to the forefront things about our own lives that may need to be dealt with.

During the interaction among the clergy working in the program, we were challenged by the group members and leaders to look at our own lives and uncover weaknesses that might hinder us in our ministry. Within the group, I shared some of the hurt and grief I had experienced as I sought to be ordained in my denomination. One of the phrases I used was, "I am so hurt. My heart hurts."

As tears came to my eyes, one of the group members said, "Even though you are hurting, the underlying problem is you are very angry." I just cried more and said, "No, I am hurt."

Some of the other group members jumped in and it was a very uncomfortable feeling. I didn't like being on the "hot seat," which is what we called this exercise. Each participant would have his/her turn. Gradually as they challenged me more and more, I got angry. Not angry with the group, but angry with those who had hurt me over the past years in seeking to become an ordained minister.

I said to the group with tears and clinched fists, "Yes, you are right. I am very angry." Anger is a natural defense mechanism against rejection or hurt. Repressed anger is self-destructive and exhausting. Anger was the root, with hurt, grief and depression being the symptoms manifested in my life. Hostile overreaction to unjust and unfair practices is certainly understandable. However, anger—even when justified—prevents effective ministering and is self-defeating. When a minister makes a commitment to Christ, she/he agrees to exemplify love even to the shortsighted and obstinate who oppose her/him.

Jesus, in Matthew 20:26, emphasized the role of "suffering servant." It was a role of honor, carrying with it the responsibility to be a servant to a suffering world. A minister is called to serve. Margaret Howe, in *Women and Church Leadership*, explained, "One of the biggest problems confronting the church is that over the centuries the role of pastor has been viewed in terms of power rather than servanthood."

Elizabeth Meier Tetlow in her book, *Women and Ministry in the New Testament: Called to Serve*, said, "As long as servant remained the primary model for Christian ministry, women were able to minister on the same basis as men. When, at the close of the New Testament period, the Christian model of servant was replaced by Jewish models of presbyter and bishop, and in the second century the Old Testament model of Levitical priesthood was applied to ecclesiastical office, women came to be excluded from the official ministry of the Church" (page 78, University Press of America, Inc. 1980).

Our modern day distortion of the Scripture has led many women to feel they are second-class citizens in the Kingdom of God. This has led to pain, hurt and anger that must be dealt with in a constructive way.

## Forgiveness

In my struggle, I realized there were some basic steps I needed to take to forgive those who had wronged me. First, I needed to recognize I really was angry with those persons whom I felt had thwarted me in being ordained. Secondly, identifying the true cause of the anger was also part of the process. I was angry with persons and with God. My actions were saying that I was not really trusting God in my situation. Thirdly, I had to realize God is always working through the actions of the one offending. It is God who is in control of our lives; therefore He has this person or situation there for a specific purpose in our lives, even if we don't see it or understand it. In Genesis 50:20, Joseph told his brothers, "You meant it for evil, but God meant it for good." We need to thank God for the benefits He plans to bring into our lives through each offense we experience. We are admonished to "give thanks in all things" (I Thessalonians 5:18). *Thanking God* is an act of our will and *giving thanks* is an act of our emotions. Fourthly, we need to discern what character qualities God wants to develop in our lives through the offense. When we react wrongly to an offense, we are revealing a lack of character traits which we need to develop. We need to develop the Fruit of the Spirit in our lives: "love, joy, peace, patience, kindness, goodness, faithfulness, gentleness and self-control" (Galatians 5:22). This fruit will be pleasing to God. I realized during this part of my journey that God was seeking to make some of these roots go deeper into my heart and life. I needed to love and have patience with those who were against me, whatever their reasons. Peace and joy were there for me to experience if I would just allow the

Holy Spirit control in my life. I was learning my lessons very slowly. God was showing me that His way was forgiveness. He seemed to be saying to me, "How can you serve my church if you cannot forgive others?"

Exposing the anger in my heart during our CPE sessions helped me deal with it in a more constructive way. To deny or repress suffering in one's life can lead to indifference. I began to see that suffering was not a punishment God was allotting me. Suffering was a tool God was using in my life to help rid me of more of the self-life and to enable me to love more fully. Suffering can also be a part of fulfilling God's purpose. Suffering produces change in our lives.

*Anybody can become angry—*
*that is easy; but to be angry*
*with the right person, and to*
*the right degree, and at the*
*right time, and for the right way—that is not within*
*everybody's power and is not easy.*
　　　　　　　　—Aristotle

## Reflections on Your Journey

Your circumstances may be different but everyone needs to take time to reflect upon his/her spiritual journey. Please take this opportunity to talk with God and reflect upon your life.

1. What areas of your life are you deceiving yourself in regarding feelings of anger, resentment or bitterness? What other emotions, positive as well as negative, might you be experiencing? Write them out.
2. List people or situations you are angry with. Explain.
3. Are you willing to turn your anger, bitterness and resentment over to God in prayer? If not, why not?
4. What have you learned about yourself through the negative emotions you have experienced?
5. In what ways has suffering produced change in your life, either good or bad?
6. What *Fruit of the Spirit* has been developed in your life as a result of your struggles? What fruit do you need to allow God to develop in your life?

*"In your anger, do not sin."*
—Ephesians 4:26

# Prayer of St. Francis of Assisi

*Lord, make me an instrument of your peace;*
*Where there is hatred, let me sow love;*
*Where there is injury, pardon;*
*Where there is doubt faith;*
*Where there is despair, hope;*
*Where there is darkness, light, and*
*Where there is sadness, joy.*

*O Divine Master,*
*Grant that I may not so much*
*Seek to be consoled as to console;*
*To be understood as to understand;*
*To be loved as to love;*

*For it is in giving that we receive;*
*It is in pardoning that we are pardoned;*
*And, it is in dying that we are born to eternal life.*

# Chapter Seven

# Change

*"You are my hiding place; you will protect me in trouble and surround me with songs of deliverance. I will instruct you and teach you in the way you should go; I will counsel you and watch over you."*

Psalm 32:7-8

Through a mentor at seminary and other people, especially my husband, I gradually began to realize that perhaps that door of ministry was closed in my denomination because God was trying to open another door (a brilliant deduction, you may be thinking). Doors do not necessarily open if that is not where God wants you to be. We can try and push doors down or ignore God, or misinterpret God's will, but then begins a new learning process. (I had accepted a position in the nondenominational church because that seemed to be the only place open for me to minister, but God allowed it and He was still in control.)

Through prayer and seeking the advice of colleagues, I realized God was leading me to commit myself to another denomination so I would have the freedom to carry out the calling He had on my life. A verse of Scripture, Jeremiah 29:11, was especially meaningful to me during those years:

> *"For I know the plans I have for you,"* declares the Lord, *"plans to prosper you and not to harm you, plans to give you hope and a future."*

My only problem with this was that God didn't say when all this would take place.

Have you ever been told by God (not audibly, of course, or maybe someone has heard God speak audibly), that the next step is to wait? That was not what I wanted to hear because by nature I am an active, resourceful person, but waiting is what I did.

My new denomination required an interview and testing in five areas before ordination. These areas were in Bible, Theology, Polity, Worship and Sacraments, and Greek or Hebrew. Thanks be to God, I passed all these tests, and was informed that my new denomination would accept my ordination from my former denomination. The waiting continued because according to denominational policy, I would have to wait until a church called me to be their pastor before I would be officially received as a minister in the Presbyterian denomination. It had become evident to me by this time that one of the spiritual character traits God was seeking to work in my life through *waiting* was faith and trust in Him. The discouragement and disillusionment I had experienced over the years had immobilized me and decreased my vision. I continued to attend a church in my former denomination, although it was not my home church. The associate pastor who had been in charge of my ordination at my home church was now senior pastor at this Baptist church, and was very supportive. Looking back, I can see that I did not step out in faith and begin attending a church in my new denomination. You are probably thinking, she sure was holding on to her former denomination, and you are right, I was. I just did not realize this at the time and I was really in limbo. God was continuing to build up my faith step by step. To step out in a new direction often requires letting go of something past or present. I found that you can't receive what God wants to give you until you turn loose of what you are holding on to now.

## Leaving the Fold

After two years (did I hear you say stubborn, stubborn) and a vast improvement in my mental and emotional state, with freedom from depression, I felt the Lord was leading me to make a complete break with my former denomination. After my husband and I discussed this, in January 1998 we began attending a Presbyterian church. I was still playing the waiting game regarding a place of ministry, but this time I had complete peace that I was exactly where God wanted me to be and everything would work out in His time. After a wait of six months (which seemed such a short time compared to all the waiting I had already experienced) from the time I actually stepped out of my former denomination, I was called by the executive Presbyter of the Presbytery of our area to preach for several Sundays at a Presbyterian church about twenty minutes from my home. As far as I knew, it was just to fill in because their pastor of twenty-seven years had died and they did not have a pastor. After the second Sunday of preaching in their church, their Session (the Session is the ruling body of a local Presbyterian church) met with me and asked if I would consider becoming their Stated Supply Pastor for a year. Well, I was shocked. The reason I was shocked was that this is an African American church and I am a white woman. When they asked if I would be their pastor, my mouth fell open and I just stood there. Finally I said, "You do realize I'm white?" They just laughed and said, "It doesn't matter to us." I said, "Well, if it doesn't matter to you, it doesn't matter to me either, if our Presbytery will approve it."

The Session of the church approached our Presbytery and I appeared before the Committee on Ministry for oral examinations and was recommended to Presbytery. Next, I appeared before the Presbytery (between 200-300 ministers and elders) and they examined me (questioned me), as is their procedure for receiving all ministers into the denomination.

When I was being examined, the moderator noticed my maiden name was "Preacher." He asked, "Is 'Preacher' *really* your name?"

I said, "Yes, it was predestined." Naturally the whole group laughed since we as Presbyterians believe in predestination, that God is in control and orchestrates life. I had been learning through my journey, experientially, that God truly does orchestrate my life, and He can be trusted.

I was accepted into the Presbytery of the Presbyterian Church, USA as one of their ministers, on June 7, 1998. It was a wonderful day. The Lord's ways are not our ways, as I have found out from experience. I would not have done things the way He did them, but His ways are truly best. It took me over three years to understand this truth from a spiritual and personal perspective. Our God is a God of infinite patience. Thanks be to God.

I am grateful to the Lord for bringing me into the Presbyterian Church, USA. The Apostle Paul wrote in Galatians 5:1: "It is for freedom that Christ has set us free. Stand firm, then, and do not let yourselves be burdened again by a yoke of slavery." That is how I feel, free. Free to be who and what God created me to be in this life. Free to receive a new vision from the Lord.

*Where there is no vision, the people perish.*
—Proverbs 29:18 (KJV)

## Reflections on Your Journey

Your circumstances may be different but everyone needs to take time to reflect upon his/her spiritual journey. Please take this opportunity to talk with God and reflect upon your life.

1. What doors do you feel God is closing in your life?
2. What doors do you feel God is opening in your life?
3. Do you have someone whose advice you value to discuss your options with? Who and why would you choose him/her?
4. What do you feel God is telling you to do in the situation?
5. Are you willing to step out in new directions if God should require it? Why or why not?

*Troubles are often the tools by which*
*God fashions us for better things.*
—Henry Ward Beecher

# Chapter Eight

# A New Vision

*"Remember not the former things, neither consider the things of old. Behold, I will do a new thing; now it shall spring forth; shall ye not know it? I will even make a way in the wilderness, and rivers in the desert."*

Isaiah 43:18-19

Leaving the bastilles of fundamentalism was a long painful experience. After thirteen years of living through the battle, I would not go back. Some people equate fundamentalism with believing the Biblical fundamentals: salvation by grace, the resurrection, Jesus as the only way of Salvation, the Bible as the spoken Word of God. They are not the same thing. Contrary to what the conservatives (fundamentalists) think, those whom they call liberal also believe in the Biblical fundamentals. Fundamentalists try to steal people's minds by making everyone think alike. There is no room for individualism. If being *liberal* means I am free to use the mind God gave me, allowing His Spirit to speak to my life, then praise God, I am proud to be a liberal.

Many Southern Baptists have made remarks over the years concerning the Catholic religion and their obedience to the edicts of a Pope. I can see no difference in that and the Southern Baptist Vatican in Nashville handing down resolutions at their conventions. In handing down the resolution against women ministers, the Rev. David Key, director of Baptist Studies at Emory University's Candler School of Theology was quoted in the newspaper as saying,

> The statement is a litmus test of who's in and out of conservative circles. Instead of building a consensus statement, Baptist leaders are using it as a club to drive out people they disagree with. After they pass (the resolutions), every denominational bureaucrat, every missionary, every seminary professor is going to have to adhere to the statement.

The experiences of these past thirteen years have taught me that God is trustworthy and that He has His timing, which of course is not usually my timing. I have learned so much more about trusting my Heavenly Father than I would have ever known if I had not had these experiences. So I can praise God for the difficult times as well as the good times.

## Stepping Stones
*Difficulties are stepping stones to success.*
—Anonymous

The pain I experienced in my former denomination has been a stepping stone on my journey of faith to bring me to the place where I am today. Obstacles are stepping stones to greater endurance and character, not hindrances, if we are willing to learn. The journey in my former denomination produced many wonderful, joyful experiences in my Christian walk and was a training ground for what I am doing today. Many of the people I know through my former denomination are some of my dearest friends, and I learned many lessons of life through the people I have known over the years. I praise God for each and every one of them. Even the friend who told me when I was ordained, "I can't call you Reverend, it goes against my convictions." When I received the Doctor of Ministry degree he said, "Well, I'd rather call you Doctor than Reverend." I laughed and said, "You can just call me Claudia just as you always have." Today, ten years later, when I walk into his place of business, he says, "Well, hello *Dr. Brantley,*" and we both just laugh.

On the other side of pain and what I felt as hurt and rejection, I can say that my home church will always hold a special place in my heart, and God has healed the anger and frustration I felt through my journey of faith. He is a most faithful God and is willing to touch those areas of our lives needing to be dealt with, if we really want to know Him and walk with Him throughout this journey of life. He changed the path upon which I was walking.

My husband is a member of a local Presbyterian church but he often attended the African-American Presbyterian church I pastored. I was Stated Supply Pastor of that wonderful church for over two years. The Session of the church voted for me to remain as their pastor for a second year and it was a most positive experience for me, as I hope it was for them.

The journey I began in 1987, when I first went to seminary, has brought me to this point on my path of life. I feel confirmed by God and my (present) denomination that He did call me to the *ministerial* ministry, even though I went though so much doubt during those early years of the journey. This reflection of my journey has led me to declare fervently that God is calling women to ordination, ministry and pastoring today, just as He has all through church history.

The prophet Joel prophesied in chapter 2, verse 28 that "your sons and your *daughters* [italics added] shall prophesy." The word prophesy (*prophetes*—pro, "before or for" and *pheme*, "to speak") means "speaking in the sense of proclaiming, or the one who speaks for or in the Name of God." Basically it means "to preach." The Apostle Peter repeats this prophesy in Acts 2:17, "Your sons and your daughters shall prophesy."

The Bible declares loudly that women held leadership roles among the people of God. Esther saved an entire nation of God's people. Perhaps some think the men should have voted to die under Xerxes' degree rather than be led by a woman. As stated earlier, Deborah was a prophetess, a judge, a warrior and a ruler and she was also married.

I believe the Word of God teaches a partnership and not hierarchical ministry and relationship, both in the marriage relationship and in the church. It is evident that women are no longer content to watch from the sidelines, being denied the gifts God has given them. The Apostle Paul wrote in Galatians 3:28: "There is neither Jew nor Greek, slave nor free, *male or female* [italics added], for you are all one in Christ Jesus."

Women may come to the conclusion the church has no place for them if they do not fit and submit to the established roles for women. Often in the church, people use the Bible and Christianity to restrict the service of women. This can limit the aspirations and vision of women which in turn crushes women's self-worth in so many ways. The church keeps women from being all they can be and thus hinders the church from being all it can be.

The church has an opportunity to redeem its past by claiming a theology of wholeness that is inclusive. The pressing spiritual, emotional and physical needs in our world demand that the denominations cease limiting the ministry of over half its members.

In 1855, Lucy Stone wrote:

> When Antoinette Brown, (the first woman ordained in the United States in 1853), felt she was commanded to preach by God, and to arrest the progress of thousands that were on the road to hell; why, when she applied for ordination they acted as though they had rather the whole world should go to hell, than that Antoinette Brown should be allowed to tell them how to keep out of it.

To refuse to allow someone to live up to their potential is a sin against the Holy Spirit, who gives life and gifts to magnify the Lord Jesus Christ.

It took one hundred fifty years, but Southern Baptists finally passed a resolution admitting that slavery and racism should not have been a part of their past and certainly not a part of the future. The angels are indubitably rejoicing in heaven.

In reflecting upon this historical event among Southern Baptists, I wondered if in another one hundred fifty years or less, Southern Baptists might need to form another resolution to counteract discrimination and prejudice. This resolution would be for Southern Baptist women (past and present), who felt a call to pastor and preach, and were denied access to a pulpit because of gender. It seems any discerning person can see the parallels to the slavery and racial evil of one hundred fifty years ago.

Perhaps the resolution will read something like this:

> "Whereas many of our Southern Baptist forebears defended the 'stance' to forbid women to pastor and preach and....
>
> "Whereas the Southern Baptist failed to support and in cases participated in opposition against those women who felt the call of God to pastor and preach, and....
>
> "That we lament and repudiate historic acts of evil such as prejudice, discrimination and pride from which we reap a bitter harvest of division.....
>
> "We ask for forgiveness from our Baptist sisters, acknowledging that our own healing is at stake; and...
>
> "We hereby commit ourselves to eradicate this prejudice and sexism in all its forms from Southern Baptist life and ministry."

These prejudices are not insurmountable, but they can be overcome only if women are given the opportunity to prove themselves in places of leadership in the churches. Education among women clergy is not the problem. A survey indicated 80 percent of women clergy have advanced graduate degrees. That far surpasses the average educational level of male Southern Baptist pastors for whom no educational requirements are set.

Comparatively, ordained women are very highly prepared, educated and skilled. They just do not get the same opportunities in job placement as men. There is no equal footing for men and women in some of the main denominations. Change is very slow in this area.

Some people claim women are seeking ordination just to be defiant. This is such a ridiculous claim. Women pay a heavy price for ordination. They have to give up so much; therefore they are very serious about their call and ordination to the ministry in our society.

It would not work if their goal was to be defiant.

"Jesus called both women and men to service in His church. The earliest Christian communities followed the practice of Jesus. In the first century, women exercised the ministries of disciple, apostle, prophet, deacon, proclaimer of the Gospel and leader of worship. Despite the fact that women were not equal and were generally subordinate to men in contemporary Jewish, Hellenistic and Roman society, both Jesus and the early church allowed women to hold and exercise ministerial office." (Elizabeth Meier Tetlow, *Women and Ministry in the New Testament: Called to Serve* [University Press of America, Inc., 1980] page 139). The New Testament presents the call of Jesus as universally inclusive. The call was not restricted by gender, marital status, race, social class or nationality.

Jesus came to *change* things. When He was crucified, the veil of the temple was ripped from top to bottom. Consider this, if humans were to rip the veil, it would have been torn from the bottom up, but God ripped the veil and He started at the top. It was His work. We now have direct access to God because Jesus Christ abolished the distinction between laity and clergy. Should not the Christian church tear down its walls of distinction and prejudice concerning women in ministry?

So, I propose a new resolution:

> Therefore, be it resolved, that we not decide concerns of Christian doctrine and practice by ancient or modern culture, sociological and ecclesiastical trends or by emotional factors; that we remind ourselves of the dearly bought Christian principle of the final authority of Scripture in matters of faith and practice (conduct), and that we encourage the service of women in all aspects of church life, according to the gifts God has given them, let them use them.

God says to His people in Isaiah 43:4-7, translated from the Hebrew, "You are precious in my eyes, and honored, and I love you…, Bring my sons from afar and my daughters from the end of the earth, every one who is called by my name, whom I created for my glory, whom I formed and made."

Jesus said, "Whoever does the will of God is my brother, and sister, and mother" (Mark 3:35). God has daughters and sons. Christ has sisters and brothers. It is time for the church to recognize this and act upon it.

Yes, your *daughters* shall prophesy!

*Life is a succession of lessons which must be lived to be understood.*
—Helen Keller

## Reflections on Your Journey

⊱⊰

Your circumstances may be different but everyone needs to take time to reflect upon his/her spiritual journey. Please take this opportunity to talk with God and reflect upon your life.

1. Have your battles in life produced a new vision for your future? What?
2. Can you view pain in your life as a stepping stone in your journey of faith? Explain.
3. In what ways? List them.
4. Do you feel healing has taken place in the areas of hurt in your life? Describe.
5. Would you be willing to go against tradition or society if God called you to some task? Why or why not?
6. Are you closer to God as a result of the obstacles you have encountered in life? Explain. Why or why not?

### My Total Reason

*My total reason for being here*
*is to glorify God by my life;*
*to grow to be more like him and to see*
*Him produce remaining fruit.*
—L.W. Poland, 1977

# Epilogue

*"The Spirit of the Lord is upon me; because the Lord hath anointed me to preach good tidings unto the meek; he hath sent me to bind up the brokenhearted, to proclaim liberty to the captives, and the opening of the prison to them that are bound; To proclaim the acceptable year of the Lord, and the day of vengeance of our God; to comfort all that mourn; To appoint unto them that mourn in Zion, to give unto them beauty for ashes, the oil of joy for mourning, the garment of praise for the spirit of heaviness; that they might be called trees of righteousness, the planting of the Lord, that he might be glorified."*

Isaiah 61:1-3 KJV; Luke 4:18

This is the calling God has put upon my life. It is my responsibility to be obedient. The hand of the Lord was upon me as He took me on a journey that would allow me to be faithful to His calling.

The Lord has been gracious to me and recently called me as associate pastor in a local Presbyterian church in the city in which I live. It is a wonderful church, over one hundred years old, with a good pastor and special people. I am excited about ministering with them in our community.

There is a little book by Bruce Wilkinson sweeping the nation called *The Prayer of Jabez* taken from II Chronicles 4:9-10. These past months I have been praying this prayer along with many other people who have read the book.

> *Oh, that You would bless me indeed, and enlarge my territory, that Your hand would be with me, and that You would keep me from evil.*

—II Chronicles 4:8-10

The Lord has been faithful to answer this prayer even beyond my expectations. He is a faithful God.

The valleys and pathways were not always easy but God gave me His grace and power to persevere in spite of all the obstacles. His grace has been sufficient, just as He promised.

Lest you misunderstand, I want to reiterate. The journey depicted in *Your Daughters Shall Prophesy* began in excitement and anticipation. It progressed to disillusionment, discouragement and depression. This part of the journey taught me lessons I could not have otherwise learned. God taught me so much more about Himself. He uncovered areas of my life that needed pruning and growth. I'm grateful for every circumstance and person who was a part of that process, both the painful and the joyful.

The journey has come full circle, back to excitement and anticipation—excitement about the life God has given me and anticipation of the ministry opportunities He will continue to open to me.

God has healed my hurt heart. He has forgiven my negative attitudes and reactions and replaced them with understanding and love. Someone may be asking, "Do you harbor resentment or bitterness toward your former denomination?" The answer is unequivocally, "No!"

Yes, I am disappointed in my former denomination and the stance they have taken against ordaining women. Yes, I think they should be open to change. Actually, my journey reveals the repercussions their stance has taken on my life as a woman called by God. This story could be told, I am sure, many more times.

Looking at it from another perspective, the Southern Baptist denomination brought many blessings to my life early in my Christian journey. These experiences fashioned my life and helped create the person I am today. I thank the Lord for that phase of my journey too. Surely *Your Daughters Shall Prophesy* will encourage women called of God, in any denomination, to persevere in the calling God has placed upon their lives in spite of feelings of disillusionment and rejection. God will show you the path as you seek to be obedient to the calling He has upon your life. He will give you His strength, His power and His wisdom to persevere, whatever your obstacles, whatever your calling.

Once I heard someone ask, "How do you eat an elephant?" The answer was, "One bite at a time." Start eating. Persevere with your eyes on the Lord your God.

*"For I know the plans I have for you," declares the Lord, plans to prosper you and not to harm you, plans to give you hope and a future."*

—Jeremiah 29:11

*"Then the Lord said to me, "I am…watching over My Word to perform it."*

—Jeremiah 1:12, Amplified Bible

# Resources for Study

Women of the Cloth, A New Opportunity for Churches, Jackson W. Carroll, Ph.D. Barbara Hargrove, Ph.D. Adir T. Lumnus, Ph.D. Harper and Row, Publishers, San Francisco, 1983.

Ordaining Women, Culture and Conflict in Religious Organizations, Mark chaves, Harvard University Press, Cambridge, Massachusetts, London, England, 1997.

Women and Ministry in the New Testament, Called To Serve, Elizabeth Meier Tetlow, University Press of America, Inc. 1980 Address: 4720 Boston Way, Lanham, MD 20706.

Women Pastors, The Berkshire Clergywomen and Allison Stokes, The Crossroad Publishing Company, 370 Lexington Ave. Newfork, NY 10017,1995.

Daughters of the Church,Ruth A. Tucker and Walter Liefeld, Academie Books by Zondervan Publishing House, Grand Rapids, Michigan, 1987.

Women of Spirit, Female Leadership in the Jewish and Christian Traditions, Rosemary Ruether, Eleanor Mc Laughlin, Simon and Schuster, New York, 1979.

Women of Faith in Dialogue, Editorial by Virginia Ramey Mollenkott, Crossroad, New York, 1987.

All We're Meant to Be, Biblical Feminism for Today, Letha Dawson Scanzoni and Nancy A. Hardesty, Abingdon Press, Nashville, 1986.

Her Story: Women in Christian Tradition, Barbara J. MacHaffie, Fortress Press, Philadelphia, 1986.

Beyond the Curse, Women Called to Ministry, Aida Besancon Spencer, Thomas Nelson Publishers, Nashville, Camden, New York, 1985.

The Web of Women's Leadership, Recasting Congregational Ministry, Susan Willhauck, Jacqulyn Thorpe, Abingdon Press, Nashville, 2001.

*Clergy Women, An Uphill Calling,* Barabara Brown Zikmund, Adair T. Lummis, Patricia Mei Yin chang, Westminister John Knox Press, Louisville, Kentucky, 1998.

*When Women Were Priests,* Karen Jo Torjesen, Harper, San Francisco, 1995.

*Women and Church Leadership,* E. Margaret Howe, Zondervan Publishing House, Grand Rapids, Michigan, 1982.

*Women in the Early Church,* Elizabeth A. Clark, Michael Glazier, Inc. Wilmington, Delaware, 1983 (page 204 on women mentors).

*Women in the Church,* Edited by Andreas J. Kostenberger, Thomas R. Schreiner and H. Scott Baldwin, Baker books, 1995.

*Biblical Affirmations of Women,* Leonard Swidler, The Westminister Press, Philadephia.

*The Parallel Bible, AV and RV,* Oxford University Press, London, 1885.

*About the Author*

## Rev. Dr. Claudia P. Brantley

Claudia received her Bachelor of Science degree from The University of the State of New York. She is a registered nurse, retired. She attended Southeastern Baptist Theological Seminary but earned the Master of Divinity degree with honors and Doctor of Ministry degree from Erskine Theological Presbyterian Seminary. Claudia was ordained in a Southern Baptist church but later transferred her ordination to the Presbyterian Church, USA. Upon completion of her Master of Divinity degree, her first ministry was as founder and president of *The Lighthouse Discipleship and Counseling Ministry*.

Claudia is married to Hugh, formerly Executive Vice President and Chief Operating Officer of First Federal Bank in Spartanburg, S.C. Recently First Federal was bought by BB&T Banks. Hugh retired from BB&T and is presently the president of the Spartanburg Christian Community Foundation. They have three married children and six grandchildren.

Her first solo pastorate was in an African-American Presbyterian Church, USA (she is Caucasian). She has also served as supply pastor when ministers take a leave from their pulpit.

She is presently installed as the Associate Pastor of Second Presbyterian Church, in Spartanburg, S.C. She also writes articles for the local newspaper and has a published dissertation. She has written and preached many sermons and has been a Bible teacher for over thirty years.

Her work has appeared in *Mature Living* and *Christian Reader*.

# *Your Daughters Shall Prophesy*
# Order Form

**Postal orders:** Dr. Claudia Brantley
P.O. Box 1971
Spartanburg, SC 29306

**Telephone orders:** 864-573-7703

**E-mail orders:** brantley@spartanburg.net

**Please send *Your Daughters Shall Prophecy* to:**

Name: _____

Address: _____

City: _____ State: _____

Zip: _____

Telephone: (_____) _____

## Book Price: $10.95

**Shipping:** $3.00 for the first book and $1.00 for each additional book to cover shipping and handling within US, Canada, and Mexico. International orders add $6.00 for the first book and $2.00 for each additional book.

## Or order from:
## ACW Press
## 5501 N. 7th. Ave. #502
## Phoenix, AZ 85013

## (800) 931-BOOK

or contact your local bookstore